COPING WITH ILLNESS

Helen Garvy

Illustrated by Dan Bessie

SHIRE PRESS

Library of Congress #: 95-67134
ISBN: 0-918828-18-X

SHIRE PRESS
26873 Hester Creek Road
Los Gatos, CA 95030
(408) 353-4253

CONTENTS

INTRODUCTION

Illness changes your life — and often that of your family and friends as well. The changes can be gradual or sudden, temporary or permanent, minor inconveniences or major disasters. Illness can create new problems, accentuate already existing ones, or upset carefully maintained balances in peoples' lives and relationships — or all of the above. Illness causes practical changes — and emotional ones as well.

Illness can be overwhelming — causing a flood of emotions that often destroy your normal ability to cope. All of a sudden you enter a new world, with stakes so high (sometimes life and death) that you can't afford to just muddle through and hope for the best. This book can help prevent you from being overwhelmed — and guide you through the maze of emotions and the minefield of practical problems that inevitably arise. Understanding these practical and emotional effects of illness can help you take charge of your illness.

Coping With Illness is for those of you who are sick, in the hope that it will illuminate some of what may be going on inside you during a very difficult time — and reassure you that you're not alone with your feelings.

This book is also for family and friends — to help them develop more of an understanding of what may be going on inside the person they love, as well as inside themselves. This book will suggest practical ways you can help. One individual who really understands — who is sensitive to the needs and feelings of the sick person and who can help them to deal with their emotions — can be immensely important.

Coping With Illness covers a wide range of illness. Some are major, others are minor; some are life-threatening, others are not; some have known causes and outcomes, others do not; some have a slow onset, others are sudden. Just as diseases differ greatly, so too do people. How people experience and cope with an illness can have as much to do with the person as with their illness. But although each illness and each person is different, so much of what goes on is similar that it's useful to look at it all together.

Reading this book from the perspective of your own particular illness — with illness that may range from a sprained ankle to terminal cancer — you'll find that some sections will be more relevant for you than others. However, I hope that every chapter will provide some new insights.

HOW THIS BOOK CAME ABOUT

The idea for this book goes back twenty years to when my father had fairly routine open heart surgery that went awry, followed by a long and complicated convalescence. Although he was usually not in much physical pain, his condition was very serious and he was miserable. As I watched the doctors, nurses, and orderlies scurry about, attending to his physical needs, I was amazed at the total lack of attention paid to his emotional needs — to what he was feeling. Even though the medical profession now agrees that emotions play an important role in recovery, then everyone seemed unconcerned with, and even oblivious to, my father's feelings.

At the time I was totally caught up in the immediate medical events, but as soon as I had time for a little perspective I realized that we, his family and friends, didn't step in to fill the gap. We were so overwhelmed by the medical problems that we didn't realize there were other things going on. For some, this failure came out of ignorance, out of simply not noticing or not being accustomed to dealing with emotions. But I had no excuse. I was then working as a counsellor at a community mental health clinic in San Francisco and completing my training at the Family Therapy Institute of Marin. Since I was constantly dealing with emotions, I should have been prepared to deal with them in the hospital setting. The first few days I was perhaps too busy and too caught up in the practical events surrounding the surgery to have time to think about what my father or anyone else was feeling. But I was also unprepared for the intensity and variety of emotions triggered by his illness.

As I looked back on my father's surgery, I wished I'd had a better understanding of the problems that illness can cause. I wished I'd had a road map, a guidebook.

Soon after that experience, which focused on a major illness, I was building a wooden deck on a house and hammered too hard for too long, resulting in "tennis elbow"— a minor injury but one that put my arm in a sling for several months. This totally disrupted my life, put *me* in the unaccustomed role of "patient," and taught me that strong emotions are not only reserved for serious illness.

The idea to write the book came with my father's heart surgery; the decision to expand the scope to include all types of illness came with my tennis elbow.

I began my interviews soon after my father's surgery. Some were formal ones with a wide variety of people and their families; some were informal ones gathered during a year of working on various wards at San Francisco General Hospital, I wrote a rough draft about sixteen years ago, but other work, including several books and numerous films, interfered. Each time I sat down to finish the book, I was interrupted and back on the shelf it went — where it sat for years. During this time, I also had my first encounter with a potentially serious illness when I discovered what turned out to be a cancerous lump in my left breast.

I had discovered the tumor early, I had surgery nine years ago, and my health is now fine — but the breast cancer proved to be relevant for the book in several ways. Not only did I learn new things from the experience, but — and more important — I also discovered that what I had learned until then in writing this book was extremely helpful to me in dealing with the cancer, the mastectomy, and the period of recuperation that followed. Although the cancer took up a lot of my time and energy for a while, the whole process was surprisingly neither very traumatic nor did it overly disrupt my life. Although I was caught totally off guard and was initially overwhelmed, I soon got my bearings and realized that this time around, because of all I had learned in writing this book, I *had* a road map.

That experience made me want to finish the book so others could benefit from what I had learned. But I was tired of thinking about illness and more exciting work intervened, so again I set the book aside. Later on a second mastectomy, a hysterectomy (for fibroids), and several family and friends' illnesses added more insights and anecdotes.

With each new illness, I regretted not having finished this book and I finally vowed to put other work aside and complete it, incorporating all my new experiences.

In the end, what began as a book about the illnesses of other people now includes many of my own experiences. I didn't begin this as a personal story and I've resisted letting it focus on that. Each person reacts differently to illness. My experiences were limited (and not necessarily representative) but I think they are useful within the context of the other stories.

Every author has a philosophy, whether openly stated or not, and readers are entitled to know what it is without having to read halfway through the book to discover it. I'm a realist, an optimist, and a pragmatist — and a firm believer that we can and should have the power to affect our own lives.

* * * * *

I'll begin by looking at the factors that affect how we deal with illness and different ways we have of coping. Next I'll focus on some of the specific emotions common with illness and offer suggestions to help you deal with them. Finally, I'll look at some special problems, and how an illness can also affect family and friends.

* * * * *

It's customary in books to thank the people who have helped, but so many people helped me in so many ways that the task is overwhelming. I interviewed over a hundred friends, acquaintances, and strangers — all of whom generously shared their experiences with me and whose privacy I want to protect. Others read and critiqued the book at various stages and helped me clarify my thoughts and added new insights. Still others throughout the course of my life helped me to see the world as I see it — to value people and emotions, to look beyond the obvious, and to believe in the power we all have to affect our lives. I thank you all. Having said that, I want to give extra thanks to a few people who have been especially helpful over the last 20 years: Dan Bessie; Brigid McCaw, M.D.; Alan Steinbach, M.D.; Carolyn Craven, Linda Blackstone, and Meg Holmberg.

Section I

COPING

WAYS OF COPING

Illness changes your life. You're often uprooted both physically and emotionally from what's known and comfortable and catapulted into a strange unknown world. The degree to which this happens varies with the specifics of your illness, but some disruption is inevitable.

"Then there's the incredible, irrational, unexplainable, out of the blue kind of surprise — that your life suddenly comes to a grinding halt." [from a woman with a broken leg] *

"When I was 17, they took me to the hospital and I passed out. I was in a diabetic coma. When I came to they'd injected all this insulin into my body and announced to me that I was a severe diabetic and that it was going to have a major effect in terms of how I planned my life and my future."

"I was in the first really deep, really good, solid long-term relationship I had ever had, a relationship I was committed to. And committed to building a family, and having kids, and being able to grow old with somebody, and also looking forward to being more effective in my work — and it all comes to an absolutely screeching halt." [from a man with pancreatic cancer]

"I was suddenly radically wrenched out of one life and thrust into one that was painful and boring and frightening and banal and stupid and hopeless." [from a woman who had sudden abdominal pains necessitating emergency surgery]

All this is a lot for anyone to deal with, but although we don't usually have a choice about getting sick, we do have a choice about how we cope with some of these changes caused by illness.

---

* Since so many of the quotations are general, the speaker will be identified only when it seems relevant. All names mentioned in the quotations have been altered.

WHAT INFLUENCES HOW YOU COPE?

There are many ways of coping with illness and we're likely to use more than one method when we're sick. We may cope in different ways at different times or we may cope differently with various aspects of it. We may, for example, deny the first signs of the illness, get angry because of a loss of function, get depressed by the helplessness and dependency, and yet accept and deal well with the fear.

How you'll cope with any particular illness will probably depend on several factors: 1) the type and nature of your illness, 2) past experience with illness, 3) your support network, and 4) your basic personality.

1) TYPE OF ILLNESS

The nature of your illness will obviously affect how you cope with it. A serious, more debilitating, or life-threatening illness will generally be harder to deal with than a minor one, largely because it's likely to interfere more with your life and work and also to create more real problems, such as hospitalization, pain, drugs, dependency, and perhaps even death. A chronic illness may be difficult to deal with simply because it goes on and on. The greater the physical problems, the greater the accompanying emotions are likely to be.

2) PAST EXPERIENCE

Past experiences can be very important in determining your reaction to an illness. Sometimes this is quite specific. Having once gone through a major illness, experiencing many of the things in this book first hand, the second time around will probably be easier. You're no longer in unknown territory. If you've been in a hospital before, you know how it works and how to make the best of the situation. If you've had a broken bone before, you know that as difficult as it may be now, the bone will eventually heal and you'll get back to normal. If you have a chronic illness, you're familiar with the pattern, even though it may not be pleasant.

Past experience can be much broader than just experience with illness. As we grow up, we develop various coping skills to deal with the challenges of life. The coping skills you use with illness are the same ones that you call on for any hardship. You can learn and gain strength from any adversity — which then helps you to deal with future problems, including illness, more easily. And, conversely, the lessons learned from coping with an illness will probably come in handy in dealing with other life problems in the future.

The experience doesn't even have to involve your own illness. Although every illness is different and everyone's experience will be different, you can learn a lot from watching how someone else handles illness.

3) SUPPORT NETWORK

Your support team, including your medical team and family and friends, is another factor in how well you're likely to cope. A good support system can be extremely helpful — both by lightening your load and also by assisting you to deal with the practical and emotional problems caused by illness. Trusting your medical team will relieve a lot of fears.

To some extent your support system is a given: at the time you become ill you have certain friends and relatives — and doctors. But you can also have a big influence on the make-up of this group. I'll discuss how to build a support network in Chapter 2.

4) PERSONALITY

Your personality will also affect how you deal with illness. When we're sick, we generally follow the same personality patterns as when we are well. Some people tend to see the gloomy side of everything, while others find the positive in any situation. What some see as obstacles, others view as challenges. Some are easily overwhelmed by any adversity; others take most problems in stride and regard them simply as something to overcome. Some people are considerate and appreciative; others are selfish and demanding. Some tend to be direct about their needs and desires; others are more indirect and even manipulative. Some welcome reality and truth; others do their best to avoid it. As the old saying goes: some see the glass as half full, others see it as half empty.

Our way of looking at the world, though not immutable, is often deeply rooted in our past. Our actions often follow from the models of behavior we observed and learned as children as well as later in our lives. We may not be aware that there are other possible ways to cope with a situation and that we actually have a choice. Our familiar way of coping is often the only one we know.

> *"My role was to keep it all going until he came home from the hospital.... It was my way of coping — running around busy with the house and the kids and all this other junk. It infuriated Jim but it was the model I got from my family and the only thing I knew how to do."* [from the wife of a man who had a heart attack]

But we aren't stuck: we can develop new and different ways of coping. Personalities don't change overnight but they can and do change. Self-confidence and active involvement in your life can be learned. The first step is to realize that there *are* other possibilities, other options. Look around you and find different models. Then you have to develop new skills. It takes time but it does happen. *Believing* you can change is the first step — *wanting* to change is the next.

WAYS OF COPING

Elizabeth Kübler-Ross, in her pioneering work, *On Death and Dying*, describes five stages people generally go through with a terminal illness: denial, anger, bargaining, depression, and finally acceptance. These stages have been widely accepted by the medical and therapeutic community.

In looking at illness in general, I prefer to divide methods of coping into two primary categories: non-constructive (or negative) and constructive.

The three principal non-constructive methods of coping are: 1) denial, 2) resignation, and 3) lashing out. I call the constructive method "taking charge."

Your natural reactions will probably include a little of each method — but I think it's useful to separate them in order to look at each one in more detail.

The non-constructive methods involve being so overwhelmed by one or more of the negative emotions that illness causes that you are no longer in control. With denial you are overwhelmed by fear. Resignation results from getting stuck in depression. Lashing out is giving in to anger.

WAYS OF COPING

NON-CONSTRUCTIVE	CONSTRUCTIVE

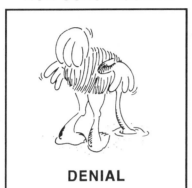

DENIAL

RESIGNATION

TAKING CHARGE

1. Accept the reality and the challenge
2. Build a team
3. Get the facts
4. Explore treatment options
5. Develop a game plan
6. Help yourself heal
7. Understand your emotions
8. Continue your life

LASHING OUT

Taking charge is a constructive method of coping that suggests ways to actively deal with these emotions and some of the practical difficulties of illness rather than letting them dominate you. Because emotions are so involved in limiting your ways of coping with illness, I'll look at them in greater detail later — and discuss ways of dealing with them. For now, lets look more closely at coping methods.

NON-PRODUCTIVE COPING METHODS

1) DENIAL: THE OSTRICH PRINCIPLE

Denial is really inaction — an avoidance of coping — but because it takes the place of other ways of dealing with illness, it becomes a method in itself and I'll treat it as one. Inaction or indecision *is* a decision.

People who adopt the ostrich principle seem to believe that when you bury your head in the sand, and therefore can't see anything, your enemies won't see you — and will therefore leave you alone. The ostrich principle doesn't work. Although his head is buried, the rest of the ostrich remains vulnerable.

Denial can kill you. By ignoring the illness, denial can cause you to forego or delay diagnosis and treatment, sometimes leading to serious and even fatal consequences.

TYPES OF DENIAL

There are different levels of denial. You can completely deny the **existence** of your illness. You can ignore the subtle early signs. You can tell yourself that the fatigue and weight loss is due to overwork rather than something wrong inside your body. You can maintain that the stomach pain is from eating too much pizza and that the sore arm is caused by playing too vigorous a game of volleyball and will soon go away. You may assume that your cough is just irritation from too much smoking — but certainly not a sign of lung cancer. And you may be right. Or you may simply not want to admit to any other possibility. My mother didn't notice a raised lump in her breast — even when it grew to the size of an egg and was discolored and clearly visible from a distance. Even after it was discovered and diagnosed as breast cancer, she seemed to be oblivious to it. That's denial!

You can deny the **seriousness** of your illness, even if you have to admit that you're sick. You may not dispute the existence of a lump — but you may vehemently deny that it could be anything serious. Or you claim the little cut you got last week is healing just fine, even though it gets more tender, swollen, and red. Sometimes denial exists despite evidence or expert opinion to the contrary. You're so sure the doctor's diagnosis of a serious illness is wrong that you ignore it. You know the lab must have made a mistake on your test results. And doctors do sometimes make mistakes — so if there's real doubt, get a second opinion or more tests.

Ignoring the **need for effective treatment** is another form of denial. "I'll just get better naturally." "My body will heal itself." "I'm basically healthy so this will go away on its own." Or you'll just take two aspirins and a nap, or say a few extra prayers, or maybe try some miracle cure you heard about and everything will be all right.

You can refuse to deal with the **implications** of the illness — that you may have to cease working for a while, change your line of work completely, or give up activities that are important to you. You may deny the long or short term effects that the illness will have on your life. You may simply not want to deal with all the consequences of being sick, and so you deny them. A bad case of the flu doesn't mean you can't go to work as usual; tennis elbow doesn't mean you can't play baseball.

"I didn't want to admit it was hepatitis because I would have to quit school and I had just saved up enough money to be able to go. I wasn't willing to admit that all that was shattered."

Sometimes even if you acknowledge the illness enough to take appropriate medical action, you may go on with your life as if nothing were wrong. I call this pretending "**social denial**."

"I try to keep up the front as if it wasn't happening. My image of myself as sickly is incredibly distasteful and I reject that and therefore don't let people know. It's kind of almost a double life." [from a woman with advanced osteoporosis]

"Even if I'm miserable, I don't want anyone else to know I'm miserable. So I would talk to visitors and as soon as they'd leave I'd feel like a deflated balloon. I didn't want anyone to feel sorry for me." [from a woman with a badly broken leg]

"I've had these attacks for 22 years. I didn't talk to anyone about it. I never missed work for it. I just lived with it." [from a woman with chronic severe pain]

You can deny the **outcome** of your illness. You may have advanced cancer but maintain that you've caught it in time and will be cured (with or without drastic measures).

Procrastination — putting off action — is a more subtle form of denial. Although you don't actually deny that there is something wrong, you take your time doing anything about it. The result is that you do nothing, at least for a while. Procrastination can be as destructive as total denial. Although most illnesses do heal by themselves, many, including serious ones, simply get worse without treatment.

Frantic **grasping** for alternative ways of healing rather than using more proven treatments is another aspect of denial. Although this grasping can result from desperation, it can also reflect denial of the seriousness of the illness: "This isn't anything that two trips to a faith-healer can't fix." Exploring alternatives can sometimes be extremely helpful (as we'll see in Chapter 3), but not when the alternatives don't work, or when they delay or replace effective treatment. Frantically grasping at alternatives of unproven value without careful evaluation can divert energy and other resources away from more productive tasks and treatments.

It can also lead to exhaustion and burnout at a time when you need all the emotional and physical energy you can muster.

Some patients grasp for alternative methods because they want painless solutions and are unwilling to accept the reality of their illness and meaningful treatment (which may entail negative side-effects). Although grasping at unproven treatments may allow you to feel that you're doing something, it may not help you regain your health and may, in fact, delay effective treatment.

CAUSES OF DENIAL

Although denial may initially come from shock and disbelief — "I can't believe this is happening to me" — continued denial is usually a result of being overwhelmed by fear.

We often ignore danger signs of potentially serious illness because we're afraid. Although many types of cancer are curable if caught early, the word "cancer" is terrifying for many people. Too often people ignore symptoms because they're afraid that if they go to a doctor, he or she will "discover" they have cancer. But if there *is* cancer, it will exist whether you go to the doctor or not. And cancer is precisely the kind of disease in which early detection and treatment can often make a big difference — sometimes the difference between life and death.

When I told friends I had breast cancer, two different women said they had breast lumps they were concerned about, but they had been reluctant to see a doctor. Although most breast lumps aren't cancerous, I urged both women to go to a doctor at once. (Even if I hadn't, I suspect the reality of my cancer would have prompted them to act). In both instances the lumps weren't malignant — and the women were able to stop worrying about them. In these particular cases their original fear was transformed into a catalyst for action. Learning that one of their peers had breast cancer made it impossible for them to say, "It won't happen to me," and that (along with the knowledge that cancer is much more treatable if caught early) prompted them to see doctors even though earlier fear had kept them from doing so.

I had another friend who didn't like the doctor telling him that because he had colitis he had a high risk of developing colon cancer and should therefore have regular colonoscopies (a procedure to examine the inside of the colon). He ignored that advice and didn't go near a doctor again until ten years later when

the intestinal pain became too great. He died at the age of 48 —
from colon cancer, which probably could have been cured if he
had caught it earlier.

Sometimes you worry that if you find out you're sick, you'll
have to spend time and money being cured. For several months
before I found my breast cancer I had been working hard to finish
a feature length film and then to get it distributed. I had neither
the time nor the money to be sick. I'm sure it was no coincidence
that I "discovered" my breast lump the day we finally settled on a
distributor for the film. That night I did a breast exam for the first
time in months — and found a solid, pea-sized lump. The ostrich
principle doesn't work; ignoring illness won't make it go away.

Drugs can become partners in the denial. They can help you
deny illness by letting you block out pain or other symptoms —
while doing nothing to cure the illness. On a simple level, you may
take an aspirin to relieve the symptom of a headache, rather than
working to decrease the tension in your life that caused the
headache in the first place. This doesn't mean you should never
take drugs to decrease pain, just that you shouldn't do so to the
exclusion of also trying to deal with the cause of the pain.
Treating a symptom shouldn't be a substitute for treating the
cause of an illness.

Of course, there has to be a balance between checking out
possible illnesses and not panicking at every headache or cough.
I'm not advocating going overboard — just being reasonable.

BUYING TIME: A CONSTRUCTIVE ASPECT OF DENIAL

In spite of the dangerous negative side of denial, there can also
be a positive side. Some limited denial can actually serve a useful
purpose and therefore be valuable.

Temporary denial can give you time to adjust to a new and
difficult situation while you find other ways of dealing with it.
Denial can allow bad news to filter in slowly, giving you time to
get used to the idea that you're ill. It can allow you to prepare
yourself inside even though you continue to deny it outwardly.
Since no one likes pain, to deny that you're ill may almost be an
instinctive reaction to avoid pain. It may be very much like raising
your hand to protect your face during an attack. As with warding
off a physical blow, briefly shielding yourself with denial can be
helpful. A horse with blinders on is not blind; his attention is

focussed straight ahead on the task at hand. He can concentrate on getting to where he needs to go. If you continue the analogy, however, and the horse always wears the blinders, he'll have a very narrow view of life — and may not see the truck that's about to run into him.

Denial may also allow you to maintain a high level of hope and optimism. You won't admit that you're ill and instead insist that you'll get better. Although hope *is* good medicine — it doesn't require denial. In fact, if you deny you're sick and continue your life without making any concessions to the illness, you may cause more harm.

WHEN DENIAL IS NOT O.K.

The trick to using denial effectively is knowing when to let go of it and try other methods of coping. You need to know when denial is dangerous and when it isn't. Some illnesses are self-limiting and, in time, will heal by themselves. Others need outside help but progress slowly enough that they won't get any worse if treatment isn't begun immediately. Some diseases, however, will worsen rapidly without outside intervention. For these, delay in treatment can mean a big difference in the eventual outcome — perhaps the difference between life and death. Unfortunately, by denying the illness and not finding out more about it, you risk missing precisely the information you need to find out how harmful the denial will be. You also miss the benefits of prompt treatment. Similarly, in the course of an illness, some decisions can be ignored while others are critical.

If you're not ready to investigate your illness right away, perhaps a friend can do that for you, passing on to you only the information you really need to know immediately. Friends can be gathering information so that it's available when you are ready for it. Friends can also learn how much time you can afford to waste and not press you until it's really necessary.

Although you may try to deny your illness, your body may not agree with your denial. It may even contradict you and force you to face things more realistically. You may go to work with the flu only to feel so sick that you have to leave in the middle of the day. You may play baseball with a sore arm until it simply hurts too much to continue.

Sometimes illness almost seems to be a message — a message from our body — telling us something we're ignoring. Sometimes the message is to slow down or change how we're living. And if we ignore the subtle signs, our body sometimes gets bolder and more insistent until we can no longer ignore it. We might be able to avoid much sickness if we looked at it in this light — if we tried to understand what our body was trying to tell us, heeded the message, and then acted accordingly. Try looking for these messages — it can't hurt, and it might save your life.

Although some denial, especially in the early period of an illness, can be useful as part of a broader coping strategy, it's a dangerous place to stop.

2) RESIGNATION

The second main way of dealing with illness is to sit back and give in — or give up. Resignation often is the result of being overwhelmed by and giving in to the feelings of depression, helplessness, and powerlessness that can be so common with illness. Dealing with illness in this way means not doing anything at all, or just passively letting your doctor do what he or she can.

Since we now know that emotions affect our physical well-being, this giving up can harm or delay the healing process. Resignation means losing the "will to live" that is so important in healing, and not taking advantage of the benefits that active involvement in your healing can bring. I'll discuss how to overcome depression, helplessness, and powerlessness in Chapters 5 and 6.

3) LASHING OUT

Lashing out releases anger and the frustration that may underlie it. Releasing those emotions may be healthier than trying to keep them bottled up — but lashing out only deals with the surface part of the problem and does nothing to help the illness.

Although you may feel better for having let out the anger, it may come out in ways that may not be at all helpful for the healing process. The anger may be aimed at, or simply land on, people who don't deserve it. You may alienate friends, family, or medical staff — all of whom you need as allies rather than enemies.

Friends can help by understanding this anger if it occurs, especially if it gets (mis)directed at them. They can also help to direct the anger in a constructive direction if it's justified — or providing a safe way to release it if it isn't. I'll look at anger and ways to cope with it in more detail in Chapter 10.

THE CONSTRUCTIVE ALTERNATIVE: TAKING CHARGE

Fortunately, there is also a constructive way of coping — one that I call "taking charge." This involves taking an active role in your healing. For those of you who want to take charge of your illness, read on — the next chapter will show you how to do that.

TAKING CHARGE — Part I:
Gearing Up for the Challenge

Taking charge means fighting to overcome the emotional and practical effects of your illness. Taking charge means accepting the illness as a challenge — and trying to make your life as good as it can be. It means taking responsibility for your health — and your life. It means clarifying your values and goals, and keeping them in mind as you battle your illness. It means taking an active role.

OK, suppose you've decided to take charge of your illness. What do you do? How do you begin? There are eight specific actions you can take.

1. **Accept the reality and the challenge** of your illness.

2. **Build a team**. Work with your doctors — and family and friends.

3. **Get the facts.** Obtain information on your illness and treatment.

4. **Explore treatment options** — both within and outside of traditional Western medicine.

5. **Develop a game plan** and then make your decisions.

6. **Help yourself heal: "The Big Four."** Pay attention to nutrition, exercise, rest, and relaxation.

7. **Understand your emotions** — and don't let them overwhelm you.

8. **Continue your life**.

Let's look at each of these in more detail.

1. ACCEPT REALITY AND THE CHALLENGE

The first step in taking charge is accepting the reality of your illness — the limitations and losses it creates, its consequences, and all the emotions it unleashes. In *On Death and Dying*, Elizabeth Kübler-Ross talks about acceptance as the peaceful final stage before death for dying patients. With all illness, including illness that ends in death, I prefer to use the term "acceptance" to refer to a first step rather than an end point — as an enabling stage, a place to begin and from which to move forward. I think of it as accepting and understanding reality. Acceptance doesn't mean you have to like the reality, just that you acknowledge it.

Unfortunately, there are times when acceptance of reality means accepting death, although even then I don't see it as "giving up." Accepting death may allow you to plan for it, finish unfinished business, live as well as you can until the end, and finally let go. (See Chapter 15 for more on death.)

Accepting reality can be accompanied by an acceptance of the *challenges* of the illness. Accepting the challenges of an illness, and seeing them as challenges rather than obstacles, then becomes part of the process of moving forward. Acceptance can allow you to go on to the next step. Seen in that light, accepting reality is liberating; acceptance is the opposite of denial.

Accepting the limits and losses caused by your illness can protect you from further harm by allowing you to make adjustments and then go on to treat the disease in the best way possible. Accepting the various emotions that will arise is the first step to understanding them and then going on rather than just being overwhelmed by them.

Once you've accepted the reality of your illness in theory, getting used to it, and its various manifestations, will enable you to deal with it more easily. Time will probably accomplish that to some extent, but you can help the process along. Desensitize yourself and others by talking about your illness, including the hard parts, both physical and emotional. Talk to family and friends — and talk to other people who have been through it.

It's natural to pay extra attention to anything new — whether it's a new haircut, a new dress, a scar, or the limitations on your life. In time, you get used to it and it becomes a part of you. You may want to show the physical results of your illness to friends and family. Some ailments, such as a broken leg in a cast, are easily visible, while symptoms such as fatigue or arthritis can be invisible to others so they may not understand the effects on you unless you make an effort to tell them.

If your body has new limitations, get used to them. If it's physically changed, get used to that. The more you adapt to your new situation, the more others will. And the more others do, the more you will. If you've had surgery, show your scars. Your fear about other people's reactions will probably be worse than the actual reaction, although it may not be easy for them. It will remind them of your illness just as it reminds you. Listen to other people's experiences. Ask how they cope with the limitations and how they handled problems. Look at other people's scars if you can — and notice that they get smaller and less noticeable with time.

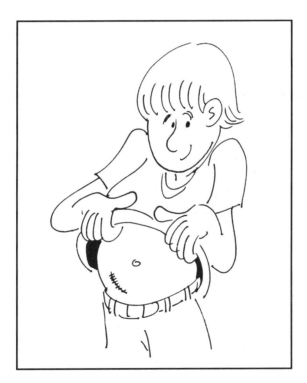

Humor is often helpful in difficult situations. It's a wonderful companion — whether it comes as the end result of desensitization or as a conscious part of the process to help you through it. Find and use humor wherever you can.

Laughter also has other benefits. It not only feels good, but with our new knowledge about psycho-neuro-immunology,* we now know that laughter actually helps our body heal by releasing certain chemicals. (For more on the benefits of laughter, see Norman Cousins, *Anatomy of an Illness*) Laughter and joy are essential in life. They may be harder to find during an illness — but maybe that simply means that you and your friends have to try harder.

2. BUILD A TEAM

Taking charge doesn't mean you need to fight alone. The first thing you'll want to do if you're sick is get help. How much you'll need may depend on the nature of your illness, your emotional state, and your abilities.

How much help you'll get will depend on the size and willingness of your family and friendship circle, the accessibility and cooperation of your doctors, the ability of you or someone else to mobilize this team, and your willingness to accept help.

---

* Although the official spelling omits the hyphens, this way allows you to see the interconnected parts more easily and helps demystify the word (see p. 49).

Look around you and decide exactly who is, should be, or can be on your team. Then ask for their help. Get all the support you need and can obtain. This is not the time to prove how strong and self-sufficient you are.

YOUR SUPPORT NETWORK: FAMILY AND FRIENDS

Family and friends can play many roles, including organizers, advisors, researchers, brainstormers, and hand-holders. Some of these may be close friends; others may be more distant. Their skills and personalities may vary greatly. Some may be good talkers; others may be listeners. Some may be comfortable around hospitals; others may hate them. Some may be experienced in dealing with sick people; others may know nothing about illness but be good organizers or experienced in dealing with bureaucracy. Some may have useful contacts and technical knowledge; others may be good entertainers or exercise companions. Some may always have cheerful dispositions; others may be realists and willing to tackle hard issues with you. And some may even need *your* help.

How you relate to your friends and family can be very important in determining what kind of support group you develop. You can push people away or urge and aid them to form a team. You can allow and ask them to help you. You can also enlarge the group. You can reach out to friends you haven't seen in a while or who were never very close. Some people may resist but others will be only too happy to help. Sometimes people don't help because they simply don't know you need them. Some will be on your team voluntarily, while others, such as family to whom you don't have close ties, may feel obligated to help even though they might prefer not to.

Your team may fall into place effortlessly or you may need to consciously build a team. Tell family and friends that you're sick and need their help — and also tell them what kind of help you need. Although this may sound obvious, we're often too proud or shy to ask for help.

There are specific ways to help build your support network.

1. First, you might ask someone else to help you do this, to take charge of organizing the support network and help with the following tasks.

2. Compile a list of those who should be part of your network. Since some of the people who come through will be unexpected, cast a wide net that will reach many people. If you have a serious illness, you'll need the best team you can muster.

3. Organize the network so you're not the hub, or at least so that all those involved can contact each other and function independently. If the network is large, make a list of names and addresses and give everyone a copy. Organize a phone tree so news and needs can be relayed efficiently without burdening you. You might want to send everyone a letter containing basic information and telling them who to contact for more information or to offer assistance.

4. Make a list of what you might need. This can be everything from advice and companionship to practical help with phone calls, medical research, transportation, fund-raising, childcare, buying food or other necessities, filling out insurance forms, cooking healthy meals, and giving backrubs or massages (see Chapter 16). Think of which friends might be especially good for each of the various tasks. Ask if they'd be willing to help you, either in general or for a specific task at a specific time. In order to be more useful, sometimes friends may need to be trained to do certain tasks or be told exactly what you need. As a start, you can ask them to read this book.

5. Explore other resources and sources of support in the community, such as illness-specific information or support groups (cancer, AIDS, asthma), church groups, and other organizations (see Appendix). Your doctor, hospital, or library are good places to learn about local resources. This task might be assigned to a person in the network.

You may have a small, close-knit group of family and friends, or an expanded one where the people don't all know each other. One side benefit of your illness is that new friendships may form among people in the network. If your support network is large, it may form concentric circles, with close friends inside and more distant friends in outer circles.

THE INNER CIRCLE

Whether your support network is large or small, you'll probably have an inner circle of people who will follow your illness closely with you and help you make major decisions. This will include you, your primary doctor, perhaps another key medical person, and one or more close friends or family members. This inner circle will be even more important if you're seriously ill and your mobility, energy, or thinking is impaired.

Some people will be consistently in the inner circle, others may burn out at times and disappear altogether or just take time off, while new people may appear.

Your primary doctor, usually an internist or a family or general practitioner, will be the cornerstone of your team, although for some illnesses a specialist might be the key doctor. If possible, choose your doctors with care.

CHOOSING YOUR DOCTOR

We tend to put doctors on a pedestal and treat them differently than we would treat other people. It's ironic that we often choose doctors who we trust with our lives with less scrutiny than we give to selecting an auto mechanic, a plumber, or a secretary. Mechanics, plumbers, and secretaries are specialists in fields we may not know much about, but we don't hesitate to investigate, evaluate their abilities, and compare their prices. That's also appropriate to do with doctors. Some doctors are better trained and more experienced, some have particular specialties, and some are simply more skilled than others. Some have different equipment available to them or practice only at certain hospitals or clinics. Sometimes there are trade-offs. An older doctor may have more overall experience but be less knowledgeable about recent medical advances and methods. There are also other important qualities such as thoroughness, reliability, fees, availability, accessibility, ability to listen and communicate, and personality.

In addition to different specialities and training, doctors also have different approaches and different philosophies about medicine. Even location can have a great effect on a doctor's medical approach. "Standard procedure" and available equipment vary from place to place, within the United States and among various countries, and this will affect the treatment that your doctor prescribes. There are often legitimate differences of opinion among doctors.

If you'll be working with your doctor over a period of time, fighting an illness together, it would be wonderful to have a teammate whom you like, who respects and likes you, and with whom you can communicate and work well.

If you're obtaining a doctor by referral, tell the person making the referral which qualities are especially important to you. Ask who *that* person would go to — and why. Get referrals from different sources and notice who's recommended most often.

You may be limited in choosing a doctor because of insurance or managed care plan restrictions or costs. If costs are important, check all fees carefully (see p. 37). Even if the doctors' fees are fairly comparable, hospital or clinic charges can vary greatly.

THE PROFESSIONAL TEAM

Your medical team will generally be your best ally in your battle with serious illness. For one thing, they've had a lot of experience with illness, so that what's new and perhaps frightening and disorienting to you is "old hat" to them. In addition, their experience and knowledge about all aspects of illness and healing is invaluable.

Although most illness can be handled by your primary doctor, some diseases benefit from more expertise. In addition to your primary physician, your expanded team can include specialists such as surgeons, radiologists, oncologists, cardiologists, neurologists, gastro-enterologists, or whatever is appropriate for your illness. You can also include nutritionists, psychologists, psychiatrists, physical therapists, chiropractors, acupuncturists, herbalists, and meditation or relaxation experts. Insurance companies often hinder this by requiring approval for visits to specialists and frowning on many alternative therapies, but try hard to obtain the kind of medical care you need and want. If you need a specialist, a referral from your primary physician may help convince your insurance company. Your primary doctor may also consult a specialist without involving you directly.

Nurses will be invaluable, either in the hospital or even in a doctor's office. They are the front-line troops. In the hospital, they will probably see you more regularly and more often than anyone else and they are a conduit for most information about you. They have lots of expertise and information and if they can't answer a question, they'll know who can.

The medical people you choose to work with may all know and respect each other or they may be distrustful and suspicious.

They may communicate well with each other or you may be the crucial link between them, telling each about the information and ideas of the others and helping them to work together. You may be the only person who actually talks to each of these people. If so, urge them to talk to each other. If you have a large team, make sure that someone is keeping track of what everyone else is doing and maintains an overview — with your best interests always in mind.

The people on your team may not always agree. Experts may have totally different approaches to a problem. People with different backgrounds and specialties will have different expertise, different experiences, and different biases. Keep their individual experience and orientation in mind as you listen to their advice. Also remember that because they are simply people, their values may differ, as well as their training and areas of expertise. If the experts disagree, you may become more confused and it may be difficult to sort out the conflicting advice, but in the end you're likely to benefit from the discussions and the process may help you decide who to trust the most. Experts who disagree might be able to learn from each other and collaborate on a plan of action. Or you may have to listen to everyone and make the ultimate decisions yourself.

Remember that medicine isn't an exact science with absolute answers — and there may be more than one good way of solving a problem.

PSYCHOLOGICAL HELP

For most people, illness causes significant emotional stress. Being able to consult a person whose expertise is in helping with this kind of stress, who can offer support and suggest coping skills, can be very important. This kind of help may come from friends or from professionals such as psychiatrists, psychologists, family therapists, social workers, other counsellors, or clergy. Ask your doctor or friends for a referral — and then check out the referral as carefully as you would a used car. As with doctors, the differences in the training these people have may influence their approach. Psychiatrists are doctors with training in both medical and psychological illness. They are familiar with and able to prescribe medications for psychological problems when that is appropriate. A psychiatrist may be more willing and anxious to use drugs to treat emotional problems than a psychologist, who can't legally prescribe medication and may rely more on talking. Family therapists are trained to see the person in the context of their family dynamics. Social workers may be more aware of community resources.

Although all these professionals can be useful, unfortunately many people don't consult them because they aren't familiar or comfortable with that kind of help or because of the cost involved.

3. GET THE FACTS

Learning as much as possible about your body and your illness is perhaps the best tool to help you take charge. This may include general information about how your body functions and heals itself, and about nutrition, relaxation techniques, and the effects and side-effects of medication. You can also learn about medical fields such as immunology (how the body itself fights off disease) and psycho-neuro-immunology (PNI for short, a new area that explores the scientific connections between emotions and the immune system) so you can better understand what your body can do to fight illness and how you can aid it. As you learn more about your body, you'll gain a tremendous respect for the marvelous machine that it is — and discover more ways to help it.

In addition to learning about health in general, you can also learn about your specific illness and possible treatments.

For those of you who aren't sick, now might be a good time to learn more about your body so you're better prepared for the inevitable occasions when you too will become sick. Prevention *is* often the best medicine.

If you're mobile and have time and energy, you can collect much of the information you'll need yourself. Friends can also help by sifting through and summarizing information, so it doesn't overwhelm and immobilize you.

OBTAINING INFORMATION FROM DOCTORS

Doctors and medical personnel in general can be excellent sources of information — and are often your best starting place. But doctors have different personalities and philosophies. Some give information freely and encourage patients to learn as much as possible, while others think of themselves as experts who are paid to make decisions for you. Of course, there are many shades of grey in between. In addition, doctors have time limitations and they react differently to different patients.

Doctors have knowledge about medicine in general, your body in particular, and a bag full of treatment skills. They're also likely to feel confident about their knowledge, which can be intimidating, especially to someone who is not naturally assertive and confident. It's important to remember that you have the right to ask them to share their information with you. Try to slow them down. If you're in the hospital with new doctors, read the name-tags, discover who they all are, and get to know them. Ask any questions you may have. That will not only give you more information, but it will also let the doctors know you care. If you want to be involved in decisions, tell them. Ask them not only to explain what they're doing but also to tell you when decisions or choices need to be made.

One doctor understood the problem only after he had been a patient himself:

> *"It's clear that most physicians don't tell their patients much and they don't tell the families much either. So unless you know what to ask, which I did, you don't get many answers. I feel sorry for the layman who knows nothing about medicine and is unable to communicate exactly what he needs to know because he has no idea what to ask."*

WHAT TO ASK

It's sometimes hard to know what questions to ask, especially if the illness is new or sudden. Start writing down a list of questions that you — and your family and friends — have. For starters, get an exact diagnosis, if there is one. If you were off-guard when the doctor first explained things, ask him or her to come back and repeat it, perhaps when someone else is also there to listen.

Get specific detailed information. You might want to know the exact location of the problem, the stage of the disease, timetables, and prognosis. Ask about treatments (see also p. 41-44). What treatments are appropriate and what are the expected effects and side-effects? Are there various possible approaches or just one accepted treatment? What might be harmful? What can/should you do or not do? What diet and exercises will help? How will the disease (or treatment) affect your life and work?

Ask how you can expect to feel, in general and with treatments. If you know what to expect, you'll know better when something is not working. Ask when and how you should contact the doctor, either to get information or test results or to tell about changes or problems. Are there particular problems you should watch out for?

If you don't understand what the doctor is saying, ask for an explanation using simpler words. Don't be embarrassed or intimidated because you don't understand their medical terminology. There's no reason you should understand it. Ask your doctor to explain any terms you don't understand. Write it down. If you don't know what to ask, try saying that — and asking them to tell you what the basic issues are and what decisions need to be made. Sometimes you may need to be pushy.

"Every time a doctor walked into the room, I bombarded him with questions. I guess I got a reputation for asking a lot of questions — but I started getting answers. I had to be very persistent and keep asking and not worry what they thought about me."   [from the mother of a child with encephalitis]

Any question you have is worth asking, no matter how dumb it may seem to you. If a doctor doesn't have time to fully explain something, request that he or she come back later or ask where you can get an answer. If a doctor can't (or won't) answer your questions, find someone who can or ask them to get an answer for you (if there *is* an answer — sometimes there isn't). Be persistent, even though it's especially difficult when you're already under the strain of an illness and perhaps also weak or drowsy from medication.

"The doctors were rushed, overworked, had no time. They woke me at seven in the morning to stay three minutes. By the time I was fully awake, they were gone."

If you're drowsy, ask the doctor to explain things at a time when your head is clearer. Schedule talks with doctors and friends at times when you're most alert and coherent. If you know when the doctor will come, ask the nurse to time any medication that may make you drowsy accordingly. Ask to be awakened ten minutes before the doctor comes in so you can prepare. A friend or family member present during doctor visits can help you to stay focussed, ask questions if you're unable to, and help remember important information.

WRITE IT DOWN

To help you make the most of a doctor's limited time and to keep track of information, make notes about what you want to ask and about the information you've been given. Make sure you get correct names of diagnoses, tests, and medications (be careful, some names sound very much alike). Write them down and check spelling of key words. It'll be important to have exact terminology and test results when you talk with other people about your illness. You may want to refer back to this information much later when you may have forgotten important details.

With my breast cancer, I bought a small notebook and wrote all the information down in it. I always kept a page for questions to ask the doctor on my next visit — and I'd enter the answers.

Ask for copies of your lab reports, X-rays, and test results. Start a file folder. This will not only give you accurate information, but it will also let you coordinate information with all the doctors involved and will let you make sure that nothing gets overlooked in the confusion.

You can also tape record conversations with doctors to play back when you're more alert or focussed. When I first met with my oncologist to discuss treatment options for my breast cancer, he tape recorded the entire conversation and then gave me the tape, telling me that I might not remember everything and might want to listen to it again later. That was standard procedure for him and it seemed like an excellent idea. A patient or family member can also initiate this. Bring your own tape recorder. Be aware, however, that in this age of lawsuits some doctors may be uncomfortable with a tape recorder, so explain why you want it.

LIAISONS

Friends can be helpful in obtaining information from doctors, especially if you're very sick. They can track down elusive doctors and perhaps have the energy to persist in getting clear information even when you're too worn out, drained, or groggy from drugs to do so. They can discover who in a particular medical system can or will supply the information you need.

If you want to have someone besides you talking with doctors, select *one* family member to be the liaison with the medical staff and who will then pass on information to others to avoid overwhelming and confusing the medical staff. Keep this person up to date and make sure they have all the information you have. Make sure doctors and all family members know whom you've selected. Sometimes well-meaning (and sometimes not so well-meaning) people fight for this role and the medical staff can't sort it out and can't cope with the overload.

ROLE OF THE PROFESSIONAL

Obtaining information from doctors raises the issue of the proper role of the expert. Although we're concerned here with medicine, the question also applies to other professions. A professional should share and use his or her expertise to help you make decisions — *not* make those decisions for you. You may choose to delegate some of your authority to them — based on their expertise and your trust that they will take your needs and values into account. But remember that the power is yours to begin with and yours to give away, or not give away, as you choose.

Doctors are important sources of medical information — but you also possess crucial information. You know what hurts, how your body feels at any given time, how it normally feels, and how it has responded to illnesses or treatments in the past. You also know the practical constraints, such as money and time, that may need to be considered. Doctors should get that information from you. Ideally you should work as a team and share the information that each of you has. Unfortunately, that happens all too seldom.

COMMUNICATION AND TRUST

People sometimes distrust doctors or the information they're given — and there are sometimes valid reasons for this distrust. In the not so distant past (and this is still true in some countries) many doctors routinely lied to patients about their illnesses, especially if the patient had a serious and/or probably terminal illness. Although this practice has largely changed, some doctors still don't tell patients the truth and some, although they don't actually lie, bend the truth to avoid unpleasant subjects. In some cases, family members even conspire and urge doctors to hide the truth.

About ten years after his heart surgery, my father became extremely weak and doctors discovered colon cancer. When they operated to removed part of his colon, they discovered the cancer had already spread to the liver and they couldn't remove it all. They told my mother and I that he probably had less than a year to live, although they also predicted he'd die from heart failure before that. My mother asked the doctor not to tell my father (who always preferred the truth) about the cancer. I opposed lying to him, but this wasn't the first time my mother and I had disagreed and since she was his primary caregiver, I agreed not to volunteer the truth unless my father asked me directly. He never did ask me, although I was sure he knew at some level and that the deception just isolated him more.

When doctors don't provide accurate and complete information, you can't make informed decisions. But even if doctors are willing to give accurate information, sometimes we're afraid to ask — afraid to sound stupid or to bother a busy doctor (and possibly annoy the doctor and make him or her dislike us). Sometimes we're even afraid to get the answer, in case it's bad news. There are also significant cultural and generational differences about what patients should know and want to know.

Sometimes patients, knowingly or unknowingly, give doctors the message that they don't want to know very much. Ideally, doctors should take their cue from you about what information you want and how you want to be told. It's important to let them know what you want. If you rely on them to guess, they may guess wrong.

After unsuccessful surgery to remove a large colon cancer, a friend's doctor talked with him about the meaning of their inability to remove the cancer. Until that time, both the man and his friends had concentrated on beating the cancer, but removing the huge tumor was essential for the plan to succeed and doctors weren't able to do that. One day, as my friend, a relatively young man, struggled to accept that he had a limited time to live, one of his doctors asked if he would like to know medical details about what was likely to happen from then on. After hesitating for a moment, and much to his own surprise, my friend said he would — and the doctor proceeded. I'm convinced that if the doctor had just given the information without first asking permission, my friend would have reacted angrily. As it was, he was proud of his ability to face the facts and the information was useful to him in the remaining months of his life.

Sometimes each person on the medical team assumes that someone else has already given you certain information or that you simply know it. Many things that are obvious to a doctor aren't obvious to a patient less familiar with medicine. When I once had minor surgery to remove a small ganglion (a benign growth) on my wrist, no one said anything about limitations so I assumed that I'd walk out, drive home, and simply continue my life. I was totally unprepared to have a large cast on my arm for two weeks. No one had warned me about that. Looking back, I suppose they just assumed that I knew I'd have a cast and so they didn't mention it — and I was simply naive.

CHARTS

Hospitals are large bureaucracies where simple routine communication may not happen as it should — because of shift changes, hierarchies, and overwork. Since medical staff work in shifts — and there are many different people on each shift — what you tell the day nurse may not be communicated to the night nurse or to the doctors or orderlies. What may not seem very important to one person may be crucial to another.

The main communication clearinghouse in the hospital is the patient's medical "chart," which includes diagnostic information, medications, and daily comments from doctors and nurses. How much your doctor and nurses know about you depends on how much they use the chart. Unfortunately you, the patient, don't normally see your chart — and you don't write anything in it. Maybe this should be changed. Patients could also write brief daily notes for inclusion in the chart about special hurts, needs, problems, or questions. The next best idea would be to create your very own "chart" — which could be kept in a notebook by your bedside for medical staff to see. Answers to questions could be kept in the same book for later reference. Be concise — don't expect busy doctors or nurses to read long essays.

INFORMATION ON MEDICAL COSTS

The exact cost of medical care may be difficult to determine. Doctors often don't know costs of tests or treatments and when you call hospitals or doctors it's hard to find out exactly what services you need to get prices for. For example, an X-ray may cost a certain amount, but you may not be told that you'll really need several X-rays or that there is an additional charge for the radiologist to "read" the X-ray. Different doctors and hospitals often calculate their costs differently so it's hard to compare them. It's also hard to know and thus compare what equipment each has available. I was amazed to discover the prices for mastectomies, radiation therapy, colonoscopies, and even a hernia, and how much these varied depending on who did the procedure and where it was done.

If you have medical insurance, you'll need to know what tests, doctors, procedures, and treatments are covered. Is pre-approval needed, and how much time does that take and who needs to request it? Will you have to make a co-payment and, if so, how much? Work with your doctor's staff on this. Although doctors offices are often ignorant about costs and coverage, once you have the information, they may be able to help you maximize your benefits. If you don't have insurance, find out if you're eligible for any government programs. Hospital social workers and local health and welfare agencies can help you locate this information, although unfortunately they aren't uniformly helpful.

OTHER SOURCES OF INFORMATION

Doctors aren't the only sources of information. In recent years there has been such an increased interest in health and medicine that many general interest magazines and newspapers (From the *New York Times, Newsweek,* and *Time,* to *National Geographic*) carry excellent articles written in easily understandable language. The *Readers Guide to Periodical Literature,* available in your local library, lists articles in a wide variety of publications. There are also health-related magazines and popular medical newsletters (such as the *Harvard Health Letter,* the University of California at Berkeley *Wellness Letter,* and *The Johns Hopkins Letter.* The *Physicians' Desk Reference* (see p. 198) has useful information about drugs; and a medical dictionary can define any medical words you don't understand (both are usually found in local libraries). Also check your library or bookstore for any recent books on health topics.

Patient information networks and support groups can be invaluable. There are national and sometimes local organizations for specific diseases, such as the American Cancer Society,

American Heart Association, the Multiple Sclerosis Society, and the Alzheimer's Association (see Appendix.). These groups can provide a wealth of information, often from a patient's perspective, and they sometimes offer support groups and help to families. Although not every group will meet all your needs, they can often be a wonderful source of information and support.

Medical libraries, located in medical schools and hospitals are often open to the general public. These will have more detailed medical textbooks as well as specialized medical journals. Although written primarily for doctors, some of the information is understandable to lay people. Ask the librarian there for help in finding what you need. And if you find a relevant article you can't understand, xerox it and show it to your doctor.

There are also a few patient-oriented medical libraries and information services, such as Planetree Health Information Service in San Francisco and San Jose, California. Now that we live in the age of the computer and Internet, there are medical information services, such as Medline, that you can access by computer to obtain information on almost any disease. Some on-line networks include discussion groups of patients world-wide who share their information and suggestions.

Introductory patient education films, video tapes, audio tapes or pamphlets that cover basic information about an illness or treatment procedure are also available and can be very helpful. Many communities or hospitals have a "tel-med" system with a variety of tapes you can listen to over the phone. Check with your local hospital or phone book. Some hospitals, doctors, and libraries have video tapes as well.

You can also form your own informal information and support network. Ask people you know or ask your doctor for names of others in your area who have your illness. Even one person who has already dealt with your illness can be a great help.

If you do a lot of research on your illness, you may actually end up knowing more about it than your doctors, who have to remember details about many diseases and many patients. And they don't have time to read every new journal article about every disease, so your information might prove invaluable. You can concentrate all your time and energy on just one disease, and on your own body's response to it. That puts you in a potentially very powerful and important position. Don't assume your doctor will necessarily know more than you. Work with your doctor. Tell him or her about any discoveries or important observations you make. Pool your resources. The importance of collecting information may be especially true for esoteric or rare diseases — but you'll be surprised at how much this can also be true for relatively common illnesses.

Make sure the information you obtain is accurate, up to date, and relevant for your case. At a time when medical researchers are constantly making new discoveries, be sure not to base decisions on outdated information. This applies whether you're getting information from friends, medical journals, or your doctors. If you have a chronic or recurring illness, re-check current research regularly — in recent years there have been big changes in tests, prevention, and treatments for many common diseases. If you have a disease that is at all rare or complicated, make sure your doctor is well educated and abreast of current research. This may seem obvious but some doctors spend much more time reading about new medical research than do others.

A word of warning. Not all doctors will welcome you as a partner. Some may feel threatened by your input, while others may resent the extra time required to discuss things with you. If that's the case, try talking about the problem directly, and ask if your doctor is open to having you participate actively in your treatment. If not, you may prefer another doctor. Many doctors, however, *will* welcome a partner who has time that they don't have to read and find information. Look for a doctor who will appreciate your input. But also respect their knowledge and their time limitations.

Now that you've finished the first three steps of taking charge, you're ready to go forward.

TAKING CHARGE — Part II: Forward!

After taking the first steps outlined in the last chapter — accepting the challenge, building a team, and getting the facts — the next five steps you'll need to take are more directly related to your illness — exploring treatment options, developing a game plan, helping yourself heal, understanding your emotions, and continuing your life.

4. EXPLORE YOUR TREATMENT OPTIONS

Your search for the best treatment can include a wide range of options: 1) traditional Western medicine, including all currently accepted treatment options, second opinions, referrals to specialists, and new experimental treatments, and 2) alternative healing methods including Eastern and other medical systems (holistic or natural medicine, acupuncture, homeopathy, herbal medicine, chiropractic), placebos, and other cures. I'm aware that my use of the word "alternative" here is relative, since many of these other systems predate Western medicine.

If you need help getting information or making decisions, ask for it. Unfortunately, in today's specialized world, it may be difficult to find one person who knows enough about all your options to be able to help. Perhaps we need a new medical specialty — a "medical consultant" or some such title. This person would be readily accessible and would know what various mainstream and alternative treatments might be able to offer you. Such a person ideally would remain available to consult with you throughout your illness — to help you understand, select, and evaluate various treatments that might be useful.

As you explore options for your care, make sure everyone you consult is clear on the established facts and test results.

HOW TO EVALUATE TREATMENTS

As you look at various possible treatments, including medications, the following criteria may help you evaluate them. It might even be useful to write your evaluations out on paper, answering the questions that follow. Write up a balance sheet listing the positive aspects ("benefits") and negative aspects ("costs"). You might also want to read the sections on risk and exclusivity (see p. 44-45) before answering these questions.

As you evaluate treatment choices, the decisions will usually involve your values and priorities (see p. 52). Keep this in mind as you do your **benefit/cost/risk** analyses.

HOW TO EVALUATE TREATMENTS

BENEFITS:
1. Health benefits.
   — Will this be a cure?
   — If not, how much time will you gain?
   — What will be the quality of that time?
2. Time, money, and energy savings.
3. Knowledge. How much will you learn?
4. Benefit to others.

COSTS:
1. Health. What are the side-effects?
2. What is the cost in time?
3. What is the cost in money?
4. What is the cost in energy?
5. What is the cost in friendships?

RISKS:
1. What are the statistical odds for success?
2. What is the research basis for the odds?
3. How high are the stakes?
4. Can you improve the odds?
5. How much of a gambler are you?

BENEFITS: WHAT ARE THE POSSIBLE POSITIVE BENEFITS?

1) **Health.** Are there definite benefits to your health? What are they for your particular condition (long and short term)?

— **Quantity** of time. Will this be a cure? If not, how much time will you gain? Will it give you three extra years or one extra month? How important is that for you? An additional month may be unimportant to some people, or in some situations, but crucial for others.

— **Quality** of life. Will the treatment improve the quality of your life? If so, how? Will it increase your energy or mobility? If the treatment gives you additional time, will your quality as life be the same as now — or better or worse? How much better or how much worse?

2) **Money, time, or energy** benefits. Will the treatment save money, time, or energy? How much? How important is this to you?

3) **Knowledge**. Will this procedure result in additional information that may help you?

4) **Benefits to others**. Will this treatment help other people even if it doesn't help you? Some experimental treatments hold very slim hope for the person involved but the research findings may be of great use for others in the future. This may be a way for someone who is dying to give something of great value to others.

COSTS: WHAT ARE THE LONG AND SHORT TERM COSTS?

1) **Health.** What are the potential long-term and short-term **side effects** of the treatment? How likely are they? How serious are they? Do they harm you or are they simply annoying? Can they be minimized? How? What is the possible negative cost to your health if the treatment fails? Could you die because of this treatment? Could you die without it?

2) How much **money** does it cost? Will your insurance cover it? If not, can you contest their decision? Do you (or your family) have the money to cover this? Is it the best use (or at least a good use) for your (or their) money?

3) How much **time** will it take (both your time and that of family or friends)? Is this a good use of that time?

4) How much **energy** will it take? This can be especially important if your energy is limited.

5) Will trying this alienate other key members of your **team** (either doctors or family and friends)? If so, discussing these criteria together may help you all understand the other's point of

view. If no consensus is possible, you may need to consider the cost of alienating a team member.

RISKS: WHAT ARE THE RISKS?

1) What are the **statistical odds** for success? Beware of statistics; numbers can often be tricky and deceptive. It's sometimes difficult to understand exactly what the numbers mean, especially for your particular case. In some sense, what the "odds" are can be meaningless because if the chances are one in 100, those are low odds — unless you are the one. And that's something you can never really know. Percentages may still offer some guidelines for making your decision, however.

2) **Research.** What kind of research has been done, and when? How relevant is the research for your particular condition? How reliable is the research? Who were the researchers? How large was the study? What kind of study? Was it a "double-blind" study, where neither the patient nor the doctor knew who received the real medicine and who got a placebo? Were the results published in a respected medical journal (which usually means that the research has been reviewed by other experts in the field)? Unfortunately some valid treatments may not be supported by good scientific research for a variety of reasons, including a general shortage of money for research and sometimes prejudice against alternative treatments. Your doctor should be able to help you understand this kind of information.

3) How high are the **stakes**? What's the down side? What is the worst case scenario if you lose the gamble? Will you die? Will you just be sick a little longer or hurt a little more?

4) Is there anything you can do to **improve the odds**? Are there more tests you could have, or any more information about you, that might change the odds?

5) How much of a **gambler** are you? What risks are you willing to take? There's no guidebook to tell you which risks are worth taking — those are personal decisions that vary with each of us. And some people are simply greater risk takers by nature, in all aspects of life.

EXCLUSIVITY

Alternative treatments can be used *instead* of conventional therapy or *in addition* to it. This distinction is very important in determining whether to use any given alternative. Any treatment that has a chance of working (for whatever reason), and is not in itself harmful (and some definitely are) should be allowed — as long as it doesn't interfere with, or substitute for, a proven treatment. If you decide you want to take the latest "in" vitamin or pray to exotic gods, or whatever, then do that — but don't stop your regular treatment and do tell your doctor what you're doing.

If you intend is to use an alternative treatment *instead* of a more proven traditional one, then you'd better be as sure as possible that the alternative is better than the conventional option.

Some alternative or experimental treatments may be worth trying even if they must be used instead of traditional medicine. If so, don't make such a decision lightly — give it careful thought and investigation and weigh the benefits, costs, and risks before you decide. Then evaluate its effectiveness as you go along and be prepared to try something else if it doesn't seem to work. It may be helpful to decide ahead of time how long a reasonable trial period would be and then re-evaluate your decision at that time.

I wish I could assign a value to each category so you could just add up the points and obtain easy answers — but unfortunately it doesn't work that way. Figuring out what to do when you're sick is a complex business, but looking at treatments in this manner should help you clarify questions, as well as point to answers.

You can use this benefit/cost/risk evaluation for tests as well as for treatments. In that case you could add an important additional question: what would you or your doctor do differently based on the test results? If the answer is "nothing," why have the test? This may seem obvious, but doctors sometimes order tests routinely, to protect against potential lawsuits, or even out of intellectual curiosity.

Using this type of evaluation may let you consider and investigate a variety of options. After your evaluations, you can narrow the field down to the ones that seem worth trying. Let's look at some of the options.

1) TRADITIONAL MEDICINE ALTERNATIVES

TREATMENT OPTIONS

There is sometimes more than one clear way to treat a particular illness and doctors make choices all the time about which option they believe is best. Sometimes they do this on their own, without consulting you, and sometimes you are included as a part of the decision-making process. You *should* be included. It's always legitimate to ask your doctor what treatment options there are for your situation and the pros and cons of those alternatives.

If the treatment you prefer isn't the choice of your doctor and he or she isn't comfortable with that option, perhaps it would be more appropriate for you to work with another doctor. Your doctor may be quite willing to make such a referral, or you may have to seek out another doctor on your own.

Depending on your illness, new or experimental treatments may be available. Some of these will be well known and easily accessible while others may be new and available only through a particular research protocol. If your doctor is up on current medical literature about your illness, he or she should know about these treatments and be able to refer you if they're appropriate. If your doctor isn't well informed, you might consider finding one who is. Hospitals and doctors connected to large medical schools are often good sources of information about current research, as are illness-oriented organizations.

REFERRALS TO SPECIALISTS

When it seems appropriate, your primary doctor can refer you to specialists who might be able to help you with specific problems related to your illness.

An example of a good referral: As soon as my family doctor received the results of my mammogram and the needle biopsy, which showed the breast tumor was cancerous, he gave me a brief rundown of my possible options and recommended I see an oncologist (cancer specialist) who could give me more detailed information. When I agreed, he immediately called and set up an appointment for me. Depending on what option I chose, and the results of more diagnostic tests, I would then also be referred to a surgeon (since my two principal options both involved surgery) and possibly a radiologist if that seemed appropriate. I saw the oncologist two days later and he was extremely well informed about all the latest research in the field and able to answer all my questions.

But here's another example — of not getting a needed referral. About a month after my mastectomy, I had a very stiff left arm. I could hold it straight out in front of me but I couldn't raise it higher than my shoulder. My surgeon recommended arm exercises but I couldn't do them. In desperation I called a friend who is a physical therapist. After listening to my description on the phone, he explained that a particular muscle which would normally allow me to lift my arm had probably atrophied from disuse. He suggested a couple exercises that I could easily do without lifting my arm, and 10 minute later I was able to raise my arm above my head. It was so simple, yet none of my doctors had suggested I see a physical therapist — and I had never thought to ask.

SECOND OPINIONS

Another variation on the search for alternative treatments, one that is usually constructive, involves obtaining a second opinion. You might do this to confirm a diagnosis, to explore different treatment options, or simply to get more information. Often your primary doctor can make such a referral — but be aware that a specialist recommended by your doctor may share his or her approach and biases. Also be aware that specialists often tend to favor their own specialty (for example, a surgeon is more likely to recommend surgery or a radiologist to recommend radiation).

Going to another doctor just because you don't like the first diagnosis isn't a good enough reason to seek a second opinion. But doctors are human and they are wrong often enough to warrant a second opinion if you have any doubts about your diagnosis or suggested treatment.

2) ALTERNATIVE HEALING OPTIONS

OTHER MEDICAL SYSTEMS

Traditional western medicine doesn't have all the answers and the search for other ways of dealing with illness can sometimes be very productive. There are other legitimate medical systems besides the "Western" one we generally use and, although they may not have all the answers either, they may be helpful.

We take modern Western medicine so much for granted that it's easy to forget that it's a relatively new science. It wasn't until 1865 that Pasteur discovered that germs caused infection and that cleanliness and antiseptics were important. Until then hospitals were filthy and patients often died from infections. Asian cultures had very elaborate medical systems centuries before the

West and they used acupuncture to block pain long before ether was first introduced in Western medicine in 1846. And the native peoples of many continents relied heavily on herbal remedies, some of which are now incorporated into Western medicine, although usually in the form of manufactured pills rather than in their natural state.

The generally skeptical medical community is finally beginning to recognize that traditional Western medicine doesn't have a monopoly on the truth about health and healing and many Western doctors are paying more attention to health practices and treatments of other societies. Some hospitals and clinics now make room for alternative therapies. Scientists are now intensely searching for more drugs in nature and we worry that as "progress" intrudes more and more into rainforests and other wilderness areas we may lose valuable plants — and potential new medicines — forever.

Alternative healing methods can include acupuncture, herbal medicine, chiropractic, holistic or natural medicine, and homeopathy. Every culture has its own system and both the old methods and new variations periodically rise and fall in popularity. While some of these alternatives are very effective, some aren't, and others are controversial or unproven. Some may have no tangible benefits but can be helpful because of psycho-neuro-immunology and the placebo effect. Some are downright harmful. Some that are useful for certain diseases are totally useless for others. Acupuncture, for example, has some very legitimate uses, but it doesn't cure cancer.

Some mainstream doctors are quite open to legitimate alternative therapies, and some are even well informed about them. If you're interested in exploring that area, let your doctor know and perhaps he or she can help. In any case, tell your doctors what else you're doing.

PSYCHO-NEURO-IMMUNOLOGY

Although many people both in but especially out of the medical community had believed for a long time that our emotions could influence physical symptoms, scientists are now documenting clear proof of the interconnections between the physiological side of illness and our emotions — and most now accept the importance of psychological factors in many illnesses and in healing. The new science called psycho-neuro-immunology (PNI) deals with these scientific interconnections between emotions and our bodies. PNI is so new that it didn't exist when I began working on this book. As we discover more about the substances and processes that make our body work and how they interact, we're beginning to understand more about the scientific basis for all these interconnections. This is an extremely exciting area and in the coming years we'll see many new advances. PNI opens up new treatment options to be explored and validates many old ones (see Locke and Colligan, *The Healer Within*).

PLACEBOS

Some treatments seem to work even though scientists aren't quite sure how or why. Placebos — pills with no medicinal value — are a good example of this. They often work; medical literature is full of examples. A simple little sugar pill that you *think* is real medicine can bring striking results. Should we ignore a treatment because we have no scientific explanation for its effectiveness — other than the still new science of PNI, which certainly explains some of it? Or should we simply use it as long as it works?

I'm a great believer in placebos. If someone can cure or help an illness with a harmless fake pill, or no pill at all, that's fine with me. And although I'm intellectually curious about why placebos often work, so that we can use them more effectively and not waste time when they don't work, the key for me is *whether* they work. If so, I'm for them.

OTHER CURES AND SPONTANEOUS REMISSIONS

Many other "cures" may have no more medicinal properties than sugar pills, but they may work in much the same way. Mystical healing, such as the laying on of hands or relying on faith and religion alone, may fit into this category. Perhaps the soothing words or personality of the healer help; perhaps just getting some attention or believing in something is sufficient to strengthen the immune system and promote healing. Medical history is filled with stories of spontaneous remissions and many of us know such stories personally, even if we don't understand why they occurred. PNI gives us some answers.

FAITH HEALERS, QUACKS, KOOKS, AND CROOKS

At the far end of the spectrum are the unscientific "miracle cures," kooks, and downright crooks. But even these can be appealing to desperate people.

> *"I'm considering the kinds of approaches to cancer therapy that I would have accepted as being quackery years ago simply because the medical establishment called it quackery. But now I don't have any alternative. The science of medicine has nothing for me except an extremely painful and destructive procedure [chemotherapy] that offers nothing."* [from a man with advanced pancreatic cancer]

Legitimate treatments that are effective for some diseases or problems but are misused for diseases on which they have no effect fall into this category. Acupuncture and chiropractic, for example have a legitimate place in healing — but are sometimes misused and misrepresented. Make sure the particular treatment you're considering has been proven effective for your illness — and that the person giving the treatment is reputable.

Some treatments are actually harmful, but even those that are harmless in themselves become harmful when they are substituted for more effective remedies — and too often they're extremely expensive.

Be suspicious about any questionable "cures" if the healer can't provide reasonable scientific data about other people treated (especially data related to your particular condition). Be suspicious if they won't explain the treatment in detail, or won't give you names and phone numbers of satisfied customers. As the old saying goes: if it sounds too good to be true, it probably is.

What's the line between treating the psychological side of an illness and "faith healing?" Between a legitimate new technique and a useless and possibly harmful fake? Between someone who is interested in other ways of healing and someone who is desperately grasping at useless straws? Before using an alternate treatment, do a careful and thorough benefit/cost/risk analysis — and remember the principle of exclusivity (see p. 42-45).

How should friends respond to all this? Should they go along with frantic searches or should they attempt to maintain objectivity? If friends are as desperate as the person who is sick, they may be just as tempted to play along — and waste precious money, time, and energy. In their desire to help, they may be overly anxious to have you try various cures or treatments they've heard of. But friends may also have a little more distance and they may be able to investigate options more objectively — which may ultimately be more useful.

5. DEVELOP A GAME PLAN

If you have a serious illness, you may want to develop a comprehensive strategy or plan of action — like the game plan a coach would develop for a sports team or an Olympic athlete.

Sports psychologists and coaches help prepare athletes for competition in a number of ways. They help visualize the goal, focus clearly on the task ahead, block out distractions, and psych up for victory — while at the same time preparing to rebound swiftly after setbacks. The same process is very relevant for illness. In addition, as with sports, any game plan must be flexible.

GOALS AND VALUES: WHAT DO YOU WANT?

In order to take charge, you need to know which direction to go in. To do this, you need to be clear about your goals. These in turn will depend on your particular situation — your options and your values. Goals can be easy to attain or slim fantasies to aim for. It may be frustrating to set unrealistically high goals that you can't attain, but if you do aim high you might be surprised to discover what you can actually achieve.

Setting goals will involve examining your values. What things in life are most important to you? As you determine your priorities, you may need to make some difficult choices. Some of your choices may be between quantity and quality. If your illness is life-threatening, would you rather prolong your life as much as possible, regardless of how you'll live it, or is the quality of that time more important than the length? If you're not facing death, you may still face similar choices. Sometimes a more drastic treatment, such as surgery, results in a shorter convalescence or fewer side-effects. For example, although both a mastectomy and the less disfiguring lumpectomy require a few days in the hospital, the radiation therapy which accompanies the lumpectomy lasts for an additional six weeks. Choices about some pain medication may pit pain relief against energy and alertness. The choices may be complex and difficult — but there often *are* choices.

To complicate matters, these choices will not only affect you, but they will also affect family and friends, doctors, and the person who pays the bills (perhaps even an insurance company or the government). The choices you make between quality and quantity may not be the same as the choices your family and friends would make. Each person has his or her own values and needs, and each has a unique personality. One person may care more about the quality of life, while another may want as much time as possible to spend with family or friends or to finish some particularly important work. It may not be easy to mesh the different (and perhaps conflicting) interests of the sick person, his or her family and friends, the doctors, and the bill payers.

Doctors often see their primary goal as prolonging life, sometimes with less concern for the quality of that life. Fortunately, the medical profession and society at large are beginning to re-examine this issue.

It's important for you to be clear about your goals and values and convey them to the doctors. Doctors should solicit this information from you and include you in decisions, but you may have to take the initiative in requesting or demanding that. For example, a doctor may want to relieve your pain by prescribing medication. It might be more important to you, however, to be fully alert, even at the cost of feeling some pain and so you might want to forgo the medication, or take a milder form. By participating in decisions along with your doctors you will help ensure that what is being done is what's best for *you* — and you'll feel more in control of your life.

CONTROL WHAT YOU CAN: YOU'RE THE BOSS

In theory, all medical procedures require your consent. You, not the doctor, are legally the boss. The doctors' power comes largely because you give it to them, either explicitly by signing waivers or implicitly by not challenging their recommendations. You can refuse to take medication, you can sign yourself out of a hospital "against medical advice," you can change doctors, or you can file a durable power of attorney or a living will to request not to be kept alive by machines. I'm not suggesting you do all, or any, of these things, but it is your right.

If you start from that premise, then it makes sense to ask your doctors to give you sufficient information to decide whether to follow their advice. Respect your doctor as a knowledgeable, experienced, and valuable advisor, but remember — it's your body and your life.

Also remember that medical decisions aren't totally objective or always based on simple facts — and that objective facts may point in different directions. What is best for one person may not be best for another. Most decisions are at least partially subjective and should take *your* needs, feelings, values, and goals into account.

In addition to major decisions, there are many secondary decisions that you can make or actively participate in — decisions relating to drugs, anesthesia, whether to recuperate at home or in a hospital, even types of bandages.

Immediately after my first mastectomy the surgeon put me in a very comfortable elastic corset that I wore for two weeks. I loved it. It held all the bandages in place and protected the operated area, so that I was less fearful of injuring it. Long before I could wear a prosthesis or a regular bra, which irritated a tiny drain incision that had been made right on the bra line, I could wear the corset, stuff the bra, and look perfectly normal. I used a different doctor for the second mastectomy, one who didn't normally prescribe a corset. I asked him if I could re-use the corset, and to please make the drainage incision below the bra line. He agreed to both requests willingly.

With drugs, there is often a trade off between effectiveness and side-effects. Some medication (and dosages) may be clear-cut. Effectively controlling an infection may require a specific amount of an antibiotic. But at other times, you may be able to decide, for example, whether you'd prefer to tolerate some pain rather than be too sleepy to think straight. You can also decide what is too much pain and what is simply annoying discomfort that you're willing to tolerate.

Anesthesia is another area where you may have more control and choice than you think. It's standard hospital procedure for the anesthesiologist to contact you the night before surgery to ask basic questions about allergies and drug tolerance. You are seldom given any choices — but you can ask. Even though you're not an expert chemist, there are things you can discuss. If you know your tolerance to drugs in general or to a particular drug, tell the anesthesiologist. In some situations you may have a choice of a general or a local anaesthetic, although you may not be given the choice unless you ask about it.

My first mastectomy was also my first experience with general anesthesia and I was so concerned about all the other decisions I had to make that it didn't occur to me to ask the anesthesiologist any details. I did tell him that I suspected I might be sensitive to medication and might not need a lot. Soon after I entered the hospital for surgery, a nurse came by to give me a shot to "calm" me before going to the operating room. I objected that I didn't need calming and preferred to not have the shot. "Doctor's orders," she replied curtly, and proceeded to give it to me. I decided it wasn't worth making a scene, and was I groggy as I was wheeled to the operating room.

Next time around, I decided to settle that issue beforehand. I called the anesthesiologist several days before the surgery and told him my preference for skipping the tranquilizer. He had no objection — and that one detail made a great difference in my whole experience. The morning of the surgery I watched as they prepared several of us for surgery. Far from being nervous, I was quite curious about exactly what was happening. When I was wheeled into the operating room, I met the nurses who would assist during the surgery. One nurse was about to begin an IV (intravenous) line in my left arm for the anesthesia. I reminded him that since the lymph nodes had been removed on that side during the first mastectomy, I was supposed to avoid IVs on that arm, if possible. He protested that he couldn't put the IV in the right arm because it would be in the surgeon's way. I pointed out that since this time they wouldn't remove lymph nodes, the right arm could probably be far enough out of the way to have an IV line. The nurse agreed to wait for the surgeon, who confirmed that he could easily work with the IV in my right arm.

While we waited, I looked around and asked about what the nurses and anesthesiologist were doing. I joked that this was so relaxed that we really needed some music. "What kind would you like?" a nurse quickly asked. I realized he was serious and requested some nice jazz. He came back in a few minutes with a tape recorder! When the surgeon was ready, they put me to sleep to the sounds of John Coltrane.

That's not the end of the story. Although the second surgery was simpler, the surgeon worked without an assistant so both surgeries took about the same time overall. Both began about 9 a.m. and lasted about 1 1/2 hours. After the first one, I woke up very groggy and my first real memory was at about five in the afternoon, with no memory of anything that happened earlier that day. The second time I woke up in the recovery room about 10:45 a.m. and, although tired, I was totally awake from then on. I was amazed at the difference. When he came by to check on me, I asked the anesthesiologist about it. He said the tranquilizer I chose not to have can really knock you out and my decision not to have it might well have accounted for the difference.

The moral of all this is that it's important to pay attention to what may seem like small details — they may make a big difference in your recovery.

CAUTION

Although taking control of your life is generally a good thing, beware of demanding too much control and thinking you're the only expert. Remember that you're a part of a team of smart and knowledgeable people. It's important to know what you don't know, in addition to what you do know, and to respect the knowledge of others. Sometimes you may not be wrong, but the issues may simply not be important enough to insist on having everything your way. If you're a "control freak," it won't hurt to loosen up a little. There will always be many things you *can* do. Since people who insist on control don't always recognize what they're doing, family and friends can be useful here.

While maintaining overall control, you can delegate some power and responsibility to others — and sometimes it's wise to do so.

BUILD YOUR SELF-CONFIDENCE

Self confidence will help as you make decisions related to illness, just as it does in life in general. Remember that it's your body and your life that are at stake. You may not have advanced academic degrees but you probably know better than anyone else how your own body works. You may need a doctor's help to understand why you hurt, but you know what hurts, how it hurts, and how different treatments affect you. And only you know your basic values and what you want in life. These are crucial in making medical decisions. Have confidence in your own feelings.

Self-confidence affects everything we do, including how we deal with illness. And confidence gained in one area can affect other areas. Someone who feels more in control of one aspect of his or her life will probably be better able to deal with another area, such as illness.

If you need to be more assertive, you can learn to do that — whether to give your opinion or to ask for information, advice, or help. I don't think anyone is born assertive. Most of us learn it at some point along the way, although some learn it earlier and more easily than others. But it's something that *can* be learned — and practiced. And there are tricks that can help. Write down what you want to ask or tell your doctor. Practice saying what you'd like to say. Write out a speech if that helps. Or write a letter to the doctor if you have trouble saying something (or finding enough time to say it). Ask friends to help you become more assertive. Check out books in your library or bookstore. Arrange doctor conferences at times when friends can be there to support you and when you are not too sedated by drugs. Practice saying what you want and need a little more (and more clearly) each time. Information is another way to increase confidence — the more information you have about your illness, the more confident you're likely to feel.

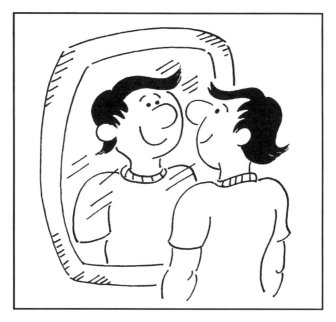

The more you take control of your illness, the more confidence you'll gain — and the more control that will let you take. We use the term "vicious cycles" for downward spirals — but what you want is upward spirals, "success cycles," where victories increase confidence, which in turn leads to more victories.

6. HELP YOURSELF HEAL: THE BIG FOUR

We've always been told that good nutrition, exercise, rest, and relaxation were good for us. In fact, we were told so often that sometimes we didn't really pay much attention. Now scientists are not only confirming that these really *are* good for you, but they're discovering the details of *how* they help. So remember the "big four" — good nutrition, exercise, rest, and relaxation.

THE IMMUNE SYSTEM

A quick look at the immune system shows one reason the "big four" are important. Your body is composed of millions of cells. The white blood cells in your blood make up the core of your immune system. These cells, originally formed in your bone marrow, take on a variety of specialized functions as they mature and travel around your body. They become Macrophages; B cells; and Helper, Killer, Suppressor, and Memory T cells.

Some of these cells destroy germs — bacteria, fungi, or viruses — that enters your body from the outside (usually through air or food). Others target cancer cells that may have already formed inside your body. All these cells communicate through a very sophisticated communication network throughout your body. We're only beginning to understand how this incredibly sophisticated immune system works and this knowledge is already changing medical practice. The coming years will see many major new discoveries in this area.

If you think of the immune system cells as millions of little people running around inside you, it's easy to understand that they'll work better if they're well fed, well rested, and not over-stressed. And it's not just the immune system that is helped. Your body is constantly creating new cells to replace those that are old or damaged. Those new cells must be created out of something, and that something is the food you eat.

When I had cancer, I became fascinated with how my body worked. I formed visual images in my head that helped remind me of why the "big four" are important. As you learn more about your particular illness and how specific parts of your body work, you may develop your own images to help your body heal. You may even want to do relaxation exercises using these images as you imagine your body healing. (For more information on imagery and relaxation see the Simontons' *Getting Well Again*. For more information on stress and relaxation, see Benson's *The Relaxation Response* and Kabat-Zinn's *Full Catastrophe Living*.)

7. UNDERSTAND YOUR EMOTIONS

Learn to recognize emotions — and learn to understand them and cope with them as they occur, so they don't overwhelm you.

The next chapter will explore emotions in general and the following ones will look in greater detail at specific emotions that are likely to arise with illness.

8. CONTINUE YOUR LIFE

Continue your life as best you can. I first mentioned this as a possible benefit of denial, but you don't need denial to do it! You can fully acknowledge your illness and still keep going. What this continuation of life means will vary with each person and each illness. For some it might mean continuing many of the things that you care about, whether that means work, hobbies, walks in the woods, or friendships. Depending on your illness, you may not be able to continue in the same way as before. But be creative — you may be able to do much more than you think.

Even with serious illness, it's important to maintain what some call hope or optimism, although that doesn't have to mean unrealistic "pie-in-the-sky" optimism. Hope or a "will to live" or determination to get better has long been recognized by doctors as an aid to recovery, and with PNI they are now learning more about exactly how our body chemistry affects that. Feeling good seems to release chemicals inside us that stimulate the immune system and thus aid the healing process.

Continuing your life will also help remind you that there is more to life than just your illness. Continue to enjoy the things that gave you pleasure and satisfaction before your illness — and maybe you'll find new things to enjoy and appreciate as well. Make time to include things you enjoy in your life — people, books, movies, dancing, sports, music, or nature. Ask your family and friends to help you laugh and enjoy life.

Use and appreciate the good side of illness and the process of healing. I don't mean to be flip about this — but some good things are likely to come out of any experience with illness (see Chapter 12). Experience, knowledge, and skills gained with an illness will very likely help you with other difficulties later in life. The strength and confidence you gain may be used in other areas as well. I don't advocate getting sick in order to obtain these side benefits, but if you *are* sick, use the illness as best you can to benefit your life. Perhaps you can also help others.

If your illness imposes limits on you, you may have to be creative. In the hospital, nature may mean being wheeled out to a sun-deck, moving a bed to be able to see out the window, putting a nature picture on the wall and fresh flowers on the night table, watching nature TV shows, or listening to a tape recording of ocean waves and sea birds.

Don't let yourself get so overwhelmed by the illness that you don't have time for good things. Go on with your life.

Section II

EMOTIONS

EMOTIONS:
Your Inner Feelings

Illness will bring up, create, or let loose many feelings inside you. I'd like to look more closely at those feelings for two reasons: first, to help you recognize them and give them more legitimacy; and second, to help you deal with them. It's very easy to be overwhelmed by all the emotions that surround illness — and yet learning how to cope with them without being overwhelmed is vital.

WHAT ARE EMOTIONS ?

Emotions are our inside feelings, our responses to things. They're not necessarily rational; in fact, they often aren't. Too often, however, we try to insist that they *should* be rational and pretend they don't exist if they aren't. Emotions are sometimes based on current reality but sometimes also on fantasies, fears, or past experiences that may have little or no relevance to the present situation. Understanding that, and learning to separate the present from the past and from fantasies, may allow you to deal more easily with the present emotion.

We sometimes confuse emotions and thoughts. Perhaps the key difference is that thoughts are usually based on reason while feelings often aren't. We make this distinction by talking about thoughts coming from the brain or from our head — and emotions coming from our insides or from our "gut." Emotions upset your stomach, make your heart beat faster, and tie your insides in knots.

Since feelings aren't rational, you may stir up emotions that don't make sense, or that seem inconsistent or contradictory. You may think those emotions are "wrong," according to your or someone else's values.   This can make it even harder to acknowledge the feelings or talk about them. An obvious example is when you feel pressure, from inside yourself or from family or friends, to be "brave" and "strong" in dealing with an illness. This implies that if you're not feeling strong, you'd better hide your real feelings and pretend, because it's not OK to express that.

Unfortunately, denying feelings usually doesn't work in the long run. The anger (or whatever feeling) may hang around, perhaps buried, hidden, or unrecognized. It may burst out later at someone or something totally unrelated to the original cause; or it may just smolder and affect everything without you really knowing why you're so cross at the world or so depressed. When we don't recognize a feeling, it's often harder to deal with it — or it may come out in disguised or indirect ways.

But while feelings are a normal part of life, sometimes when you're sick the emotions are so powerful that, instead of co-existing with and complementing the rational part of you, they dominate everything else. The result is that you may become so overwhelmed and immobilized by these feelings that you become their prisoner. When you feel these emotions with such intensity, perhaps for the first time, you can easily feel a little crazy. Don't worry; it's normal.

My goal in looking closely at feelings is not to make them disappear (though some may be altered) but to help get them out in the open. By examining feelings, you can prevent them from immobilizing you, and you have a greater chance of staying in control of your life.   While you may not be able to control your feelings, you *can* control what you do about them.

HOW ILLNESS AFFECTS EMOTIONS

Illness affects your emotions in several ways. First, it creates a lot of change and disruption that you have to adjust to — and which is likely to cause emotional reactions. Second, it lowers your natural defenses that may previously have successfully blocked the emotions or allowed you to cope with them effortlessly.

Some people aren't used to noticing, acknowledging, or sharing their feelings, and the obvious, undeniable presence of emotions may itself be a new experience.

"I'm so used to repressing my own emotions. I'm used to hiding them, even from myself."

"I became more open with people and said what I was feeling. My feelings were more on the surface than normal. My son came to see me and when he left I started to cry. My mother walked in just then and said, 'John, you're crying.' That was the first time in 40 years and I said, 'Yes, isn't it about time?'"

A fifty year old man told me:

"Emotions? Before this illness I don't think I knew I had them."

This same man later went on to say that learning to recognize, express, and accept his emotions was one of the great benefits of his illness.

Others are perhaps more familiar or comfortable with feelings in general but may be totally unprepared for certain particular feelings. One woman didn't know what to do when her husband became depressed during a major illness.

"Kevin got really depressed after his heart attack. I had no idea of what depression was; I've always been a very even keel person. I had no understanding and nobody to give me help with it. It was an incredibly scary time."

Illness lowers your resistance, not just physically but also emotionally, so that feelings that you might have easily handled before the illness all of a sudden become overpowering.

"I was feeling at the rock bottom of vulnerability — touch me and I'll cry."

"When you're ill, minor things completely freak you out. I can't get a pain anywhere else without worrying. I had canker sores all over my gums and I freaked out. You get freaked out by things you can handle ordinarily."

"There are times when I have come close to breaking under this illness, psychologically just having a complete nervous breakdown — like losing things, the house getting completely disorganized. There are times when I have let everything go and I feel very close to the edge, almost needing hospitalization mentally."

"There was a period of a couple years where I thought I was stark raving mad. I was doing the most irrational things."

Since you're primarily focussed on the physical symptoms of your illness, you may not realize that all these changes are related to it. You may be disturbed, confused, or even frightened by the new feelings.

THE ROLLER COASTER

A serious illness can be like riding a roller coaster. You may feel you're on a track you can't control, with slow climbs and terrifying plunges — and every time you begin to catch your breath, there's another twist or turn. You may constantly be surprised with new information, new test results, new prognoses, new treatments to try, new directions to go in. It can make you dizzy. Your emotions may go up and down, responding to each new twist in the illness, each new piece of news. You may need to re-adjust your master plan often — with each new turn bringing up yet another emotion. All this makes it more difficult to deal with your emotions as you and they speed around on the roller coaster.

Since there may be no way to get off the roller coaster, my best advice is to sit back, hold on, take a deep breath, brace yourself for the inevitable ups and downs — and stay flexible enough to adjust.

HOW TO DEAL WITH EMOTIONS

So, what should you do with all those feelings? The four main things you can do are: 1) recognize and acknowledge the feelings, 2) talk about them, 3) check out the reality of the situation, and 4) take positive actions to change the underlying conditions that led to the feelings in the first place.

HOW TO DEAL WITH EMOTIONS

1. Recognize and acknowledge your feelings.
2. Talk about them.
3. Check out the reality of the situation.
4. Take positive actions to change the underlying conditions.

---

1) RECOGNIZE AND ACKNOWLEDGE YOUR FEELINGS

The first step in dealing with a particular emotion is to recognize and acknowledge it.

Perhaps you think of emotions as unwelcome strangers, intruders, or enemies to be pushed away or hidden. I hope you'll begin to see them as more neutral, as normal parts of yourself, as acquaintances or perhaps even friends. I hope you'll understand that emotions are real and legitimate parts of you — parts that make up the whole you. You should also know that most other people have these same feelings — you're not alone. And you're definitely not "weird" or crazy for having them.

2) TALK ABOUT YOUR FEELINGS

When feelings are overwhelming or frightening, talking about them and about your illness is usually helpful. Talking can serve many purposes. Just talking about a problem sometimes seems to make it disappear, or at least shrink to a more manageable size as you define and examine it. Talking lets you explore various aspects of your feelings, and that increased clarity may be useful in separating out what parts are really connected to the present situation and what parts involve past experiences, fears, or fantasies. In addition, talking can simply "let off steam."

A funny thing happens with emotions — the more you share yours with other people, the better they get to know you and the more they're likely to open up and show you their emotions. That process usually leads to better understanding of each other and to increased closeness and intimacy.

Talking with family and friends is wonderful. But if that's difficult or if they can't meet your needs, there are professionals who have had a lot of experience with those kinds of feelings and who are trained to help you explore your feelings and deal with them — psychologists, family therapists, psychiatrists, social workers, and sometimes clergy. Seek out people in these fields who are experienced in dealing with illness — perhaps even your particular illness. Support groups of other people with the same disease can also be helpful. Find people who will listen to you.

"What helped us was that we started reaching out to people and telling them about our fears and so forth. That helped. It's all so simple once you can talk about it. We needed a therapist, we couldn't just do it ourselves." [from a woman whose husband had a heart attack]

"I wish there was more chance to talk to someone who wasn't a member of the family, that you didn't have to put up a front for. You don't want to dump on your family."

When talking with friends and family, know what you want from them. Do you just want to talk in order to air your feelings or to think out loud? Or do you want information, advice, feedback, or help? Or do you just want someone to sit quietly with you, listen, and hold your hand? Let them know clearly what you want and need.

It's important to be able to talk about what's really going on inside you and to do so directly. That means you have to become vulnerable to some extent. You have to face the fear that others will reject you in some way because of your feelings. That's the risk. But remember that although specific feelings will differ, *everyone* has feelings. The differences are part of what makes each of us unique. And sharing those feelings will generally increase closeness and understanding.

As you learn to deal with your emotions, perhaps you can help your friends and family to deal with theirs. That, in turn, may help you, since people sometimes stay away because they don't know how to deal with the emotions illness brings on.

LAYERS OF EMOTIONS

Sometimes one emotion can hide others. Talking may enable the top layers to be peeled back to expose the ones underneath. Anger, for example, may mask helplessness, frustration, or fear. The more you can peel back the layers, the more likely you are to get to the core, the most hidden emotions. Once they're out in the open, you can begin to deal with them.

LISTENING: A WORD FOR FAMILY AND FRIENDS

Communication is more than just talking — it's a two-part process. One person talks and the other listens. If you're a friend, you can help someone who's sick by being available and willing to listen. It helps to know what the sick person wants from you, so if you're not sure, ask. It can also help to set aside expectations or preconceived notions about what the other person feels. Tell the sick person you really want to know what they're feeling and thinking — whatever it is. Take your cues from them. Although gentle probing questions sometimes work, don't force someone to talk when they're not ready. Remember that you don't have to agree — it's sufficient to listen and try to understand.

Friends' attitudes can be important. Often visitors think their role is to cheer up the patient. But that only makes it harder for the sick person to talk about certain kinds of feelings. What if the patient wants to talk about death, or pain, or medical bills? To reply, "Don't worry about that" only closes the door and may give the message that you aren't comfortable talking about those topics. Try not to impose a cheerfulness that leaves no room to talk about negative feelings — but, on the other hand, don't present such a gloomy attitude that there's no room for joy or laughter.

Sometimes people who are sick just don't want to talk about their illness because they're tired of focussing on it, rather than because they want to hide the feelings. In order to feel like they're still part of the outside world, they may want to talk about the things they used to talk about with you before they got sick. And constantly talking about illness can get boring.

If you're a friend or family member, remember that some of us have trouble just listening. If we hear a problem, we feel we have to resolve it. If this applies to you — relax. Often it's enough just to listen. Let the sick person ask if he or she wants help with solutions. Of course you can offer to help if you see something you could do, but listening doesn't automatically make you responsible for solving the problem.

COMMUNICATIONS PROBLEMS

Talking isn't always an easy process. As you talk and friends listen, they filter your words through *their* experiences, *their* biases and values, and *their* feelings so that in the end what they hear may not be what you said. That leaves many opportunities for miscommunication. Simply being aware of this may help but it's also a situation where therapists can be useful.

Certain specific problems can hamper communications, such as patients who can't talk because they are on respirators or are heavily sedated, and the very young or very old who can't talk or communicate clearly. These require patience and creativity.

Sometimes communication suffers because you and your family and friends aren't on the same wavelength, aren't talking in the same terms. This can be due to different values and goals, different needs, different information or assumptions, or different ways of coping. Talking can often clarify these differences, which may then lead to better understanding.

Differences in information can be accidental or deliberate; for example, when a doctor tells the family the truth but is less than completely honest with the patient. Or the doctor may have given the same information but each person *heard* it differently.

3) CHECK OUT REALITY

Although emotions don't necessarily reflect reality — it's important to be aware of the reality of the situation. It's not wrong to think about death, for example, if you aren't objectively in danger of dying — we all worry about death sometimes. But it's important to be aware of the reality in order to take the next step.

If feelings and reality are different, it's important to be clear about reality before making decisions. If you're unsure about the reality, talking may help clarify it. Ask friends or your doctor to help.

If you're a friend, you may have information or simply a distance and perspective that the person who is sick lacks. Beware, however, of glossing over real problems.

Although the attempt to make emotions rational can be useful, it can also take away from their validity, so be careful not to invalidate feelings in your attempt to interject reality.

4) TAKE POSITIVE ACTIONS

There are almost always positive actions you can take to change the underlying conditions that led to a particular feeling. Since feelings aren't rational, this won't necessarily make them disappear, but it can help. I'll look at this more closely in relation to specific emotions in the following chapters.

Involve your whole team. Many people brainstorming and actively working to solve specific problems will be more likely to find solutions than will a single person sitting and worrying alone, or even several people siting and worrying separately.

THE NEGATIVE EMOTIONS OF ILLNESS

In the following seven chapters I'll look closely at the most important negative emotions caused by illness and suggest ways of dealing with each of them. These emotions are all perfectly normal, common reactions to illness. The primary emotions I'll examine are:

1) powerlessness, helplessness, and dependency;
2) depression;
3) worthlessness;
4) fear;
5) loneliness;
6) anger;
7) guilt.

If you're sick, a lot of these may be difficult emotions to read about and to think about logically. Taken all at once, it may seem overwhelming and even depressing. If so, skip these chapters. You may want to come back to them later, as certain specific emotions crop up — or you may want to read them piecemeal, at a rate you can absorb. If, as with some people, you feel a lot of churning inside but aren't sure what it is, read on — you may find some of these emotions familiar.

For those who are sick, much of this section may seem pretty obvious, and it is — except perhaps when you're in the middle of it and everything feels like one big muddle. For that reason it may help to examine each emotion separately. For each emotion, I'll first look at the emotion and its causes and then suggest specific things you can do to begin changing some of those feelings. This will then free you up to deal better with the illness itself.

The following chapters may also be useful for friends and family — to help them understand some of the feelings that may be going on inside you. Reading this may help you to all talk together about those feelings. Friends should also see Chapter 16.

And don't despair, there are also *positive* emotions that come from illness. I'll discuss those in Chapter 12.

POWERLESSNESS AND DEPENDENCY

"I felt powerless, helpless, and hopeless."

This powerlessness is primarily caused by: 1) the deluge of emotions, practical problems, and decisions that descend on you when you become sick; 2) not being in control, 3) being dependent on other people, which in turn comes from the loss of mobility and function due to the illness; and 4) a lack of information to enable you to deal with the illness.

1. THE DELUGE

When you're seriously ill, the sheer quantity of emotions, decisions, and tasks to be done may leave you dazed and confused about how or where to begin. This can make you feel powerless and out of control.

"I felt really overwhelmed, like I couldn't cope with anything."

This deluge is especially strong when you first become ill or first receive a diagnosis — but it can continue unabated as you struggle to deal with all the information you have to digest, the decisions to make, tests and treatments to undergo, and the strong emotions swirling around inside.

2. LOSS OF CONTROL

When you're sick, your body is doing things you don't want it to do — it's not taking orders from your head. You're not in control at a very basic level. In addition, your needs and the limitations of your illness often determine your actions — and doctors, not you, often make many or most of the required decisions. You didn't choose to be sick — but you're no longer in control of your life.

Losing control is hard to accept, especially for those used to being in control of their lives and their bodies.

"I give myself over to these people and submit my body to these proceedings. Submitting to someone else's control is a real scary thing to do."

Hospital procedures can add to the feeling of powerlessness and lack of control. The medical staff or hospital routine determine when you wake up, when and what you eat, when you take your pills and which you take, when you have visitors, and sometimes which visitors are allowed (sometimes no young children or only immediate family in intensive care units) and how you can visit with them. You don't choose your hospital roommate — or *their* friends, noise level, or lifestyle. Some staff members and hospitals allow more flexibility than others but institutional routine generally doesn't leave much room for individual choices.

3. DEPENDENCY

Illness will make you feel dependent, no matter how self-sufficient you normally are. The degree of dependence will depend on the nature of the illness — and on your personality.

"The helplessness was really terrible. Something was hurting and I kept thinking, 'Oh my god, I can't get out of bed, I can't do for myself, I can't fix myself.' I had to get somebody to help me roll over, to go to the bathroom. That's really horrible."
[from a woman in the hospital with a badly broken leg]

"I got totally freaked out. I couldn't believe the utter dependency, not being able to do anything or make any decisions."

"So here I was in the hospital, taking lots of drugs, and I was on 'ABR,' absolute bed rest, which means not getting up even to go to the bathroom. That was in some ways the hardest thing for me. It was horrible — it meant having to ask for absolutely everything. If something was out of my reach, I had to ring for a nurse."

Being dependent can mean many things. The needs may be very mechanical and mundane, such as needing someone to cook for you, go to the store, tie your shoes, wash or brush your hair, bring your medication, or empty the bedpan. If you normally live alone but are temporarily hospitalized, you may need someone to feed your cat, take in the mail, water the plants, and pay some bills. If you're a single parent, you may need someone to care for your children. You may need financial assistance, help in getting information, or help making decisions. Or you may just need someone to be there, to hold your hand and listen to you. You don't realize how many things you need until you can't do them yourself.

"Before Tom went off this morning, he'd built a fire and brought in some wood, but we used up all the wood right away. The gas man came to read the meter and I asked him to bring in some wood —otherwise I'd have gotten really cold."

Her young daughter quickly added:

"And I got him to get down the cat food from the top shelf so I could feed the cat."

Being dependent on other people (relatives, friends, or nurses) means that you often have to depend on their schedules, their priorities, and even their tastes. You eat what they'll cook for you, you go places when they can take you, you must sometimes wait to go to the bathroom until they can bring you the bedpan or help you out of bed. You may wait for pain medication or for a friendly chat until they have time for it. You may have to wait to have someone scratch an itch or turn out your light. You may have to wear clothes or eat food that they choose for you. Dependency can range from inconvenience and annoyance to sheer agony.

But being dependent means more than that — it means having to ask people for things, waiting for them to come and offer without your asking, or simply doing without when it's too difficult to ask.

"In the hospital I missed doing what I wanted to do. I couldn't read, I couldn't walk out on a nice day. If I wanted something I had to wait until someone came or call them up. It's not my nature to ask someone to do something. It's hard for me to ask."

"It would be nice to have more awareness on everyone's part that the sick person can't do silly little things like carry a glass of water. And to provide those services without having to be asked. I have to tell people to bring me this and bring me that and they get pissed. It gets harder to ask someone to do the same thing over and over."

When your illness makes you dependent on other people, it may be hard to ask for more than absolutely essential needs. You learn to prioritize your needs. If you call a nurse for something as trivial as opening a window, perhaps he or she will ignore you when you have a more urgent need.

When you're sick, you're often dependent on a medical system that tends to reward "niceness" and punish "assertiveness," especially when the latter requires more work on the part of the staff.

"I reach out, I'm friendly, but I know that one reason I'm so friendly is that I learned right away that if one is to receive any care at all in a hospital one has to be friendly. You have to pretend, even if you're not feeling well, to feel well enough to smile at the nurse, to greet the orderly, to thank the nutritionist."

Hospitals have paid staff to take care of you but at home, although you may have a nurse or aide who is paid to assist you, more often you'll be totally dependent on friends and family or volunteers from some organization.

"It meant being very dependent not on nurses who were being paid for it but on friends and family. Friends got together and they organized rotating shifts. There was a sign-up sheet and there was always someone in the house to take care of me. But it was impossible. There's only so much that people can do outside of a hospital."

I asked one man what it was like for him to have to ask for so much from his friends and family.

"It's not pleasant. I don't like it. I've never asked in my life but lately I've had to. It's been the hardest thing on me. I've always done it all myself. I have a very difficult time. It's hard on me but I'm slowly doing it."

You may be afraid you'll wear out your friends. And the reality is that friends *may* get worn out. There's sometimes a fine line between letting willing friends take care of you so you can heal, and not demanding too much. If this seems to be a problem, talk about it with your family and friends. If you're a friend or relative, try to be aware of that possibility and take care of yourself in order to prevent fatigue and burnout, and the resentment that may accompany it (see Chapter 16).

Some people are able to ask for help easily while others have a difficult time even if their need is legitimate. These people may ask for very little or apologize constantly. Others may abuse the situation — running nurses or friends and family ragged with constant demands, thus creating resentment. When you do need things, you're likely to get better results by asking directly, although sometimes people resort to anger, manipulation, bribery, or whining.

"I was impossible. I was crazy. I was totally demanding. I wanted things exactly as they had been in the hospital."

One woman's helplessness and powerlessness came out in her dreams:

"I had these really strange dreams. In the dreams, I'm always walking around the streets of San Francisco with this broken leg and either my cast had fallen off or I'd forgotten my crutches

and, oh, it's terrifying. In other dreams I'm always far from home and trying real hard to get home. I can't get help and I don't know what to do except to start hopping. It's always in the middle of Market Street with all the traffic."

Some people are able to look at the helplessness with a touch of humor, even though at times it's not at all funny.

"Silly things happen. You drop something and you can't pick it up and you end up making a big mess over some little thing. One night I spilled the bedpan in bed and had to sleep in wet sheets all night and it was horrible. I was super embarrassed."

Although this was said with a laughing tone, I'm sure the person wasn't laughing when she was lying in bed with wet and smelly sheets. Laughter often helps us tolerate difficult situations.

LOSS OF MOBILITY AND FUNCTION

Loss of mobility or function may affect your ability to perform routine tasks, thereby making you more dependent. It can mean having to walk more slowly; not being able to drive, cook, or do simple tasks around the house; or not being able to get out of bed or even turn over in bed by yourself.

"There I was, both legs in traction, a head brace, and limited use of my left arm. About all I could do by myself was sip water through a long tube and push the button to call the nurse — as long as the straw and the button were within reach."

That's clearly disabling, but the following are quotes from people who had fairly routine broken legs or arms.

"I didn't expect it to be so ridiculous. I feel silly all the time. I can't even carry a glass of water with the crutches. I can't figure out how to get up or bend down."

"I couldn't even get up the stairs on the bus with my bulky cast so I had to be driven everywhere — and there were only certain cars I could fit into."

"The cast is just so heavy — I get worn out dragging it around."

Casts, of course, aren't the only thing that affect mobility. Some people have to stay connected to machines, oxygen tanks, or intravenous bottles with food or medicine. And some are simply too weak to go far. If you're confined to a wheelchair you'll discover that although public access has improved in recent years, it's still far from satisfactory.

Joint or muscle problems, such as arthritis, can be equally debilitating, even though they're less visible. The loss of ability to do normal everyday tasks such as button a shirt, tie a shoelace, brush your hair, open a jar or a door can be as destructive to your ability to function normally as more major or more visible problems.

Simple fatigue from an illness can greatly affect your life — as can side-effects of many of the drugs that you may need to take. If the drugs limit your ability to drive, read, or think clearly, you'll certainly be more dependent on others.

Marvels of medical technology, which save lives, can also create dependency. Although respirators help people breathe, they also prevent people from speaking since a tube is inserted through the mouth, nose, or a hole in the throat. So someone who might normally be able to say what he or she wants and needs, and what hurts, now can't talk. Sometimes the patient is well enough to write, but writing is slow and frustrating for all but basic communication — and it requires someone willing and able to read the notes.

The first few days following his heart surgery, my father was so weak that just staying awake was an effort. But when he was finally well enough to want to talk, he couldn't because he was on a respirator. To make matters worse, a poorly inserted IV tube left him with a swollen right hand. Writing with his left hand was a tremendous effort and he could only manage to write 1-2 short sentences at a time, many of which were such scribbles that even I couldn't decipher them. For several days this was his only communication with the world.

Years later a nurse told me that in such cases they usually use a chart with letters on it so the patient can point to the letters. My father could easily have done that, but during those weeks when communication was so precious and so difficult no one suggested it. It would have been so simple.

This slow communication process is especially frustrating in hospitals. Friends and family may have the patience to wait for words to be laboriously written but doctors and nurses are in a hurry. And it's sometimes necessary to know the patient well in order to decipher cryptic communication.

And, of course, you must know how to write — which isn't true for young children — or the many adults who are illiterate. Friends and family can obviously be useful if they have the time to help the patient communicate. Language barriers, of course, also create problems.

Those who need care even when they're well, such as the very young and the very old, will be even more dependent when they're sick.

4. INADEQUATE INFORMATION

Lack of information contributes to powerlessness. You may not have adequate information to understand what's happening and to make the decisions that need to be made about your illness.

"It feels like being out in a wilderness someplace with no guide-posts at all and having to make decisions about what's best to do."

When you're sick you may need to learn and process a lot of complicated information very quickly. When you don't have the information you need to participate in decisions, you have to rely on others.

The helplessness is intensified when not only do *you* not know or understand what's going on with your body, but it seems the doctors don't either.

"I'm under the care of a doctor who does believe there's something organically wrong but is baffled as to what it is. She's done a number of tests for all kinds of weird things and sent me to specialists. She's taking it very seriously, but she doesn't know what to do about it."

One man talked of his frustration with his wife's illness.

"She's a doctor and ... if the doctor can't heal herself, who can. It's really quite threatening."

Although the next man's perception was perhaps colored by his anger and his frustration at not getting better (he had a type of cancer for which medical science had no cure at that time), his feelings are still valid.

"You have to cope with the realization that your doctors don't know a damn thing — that about this disease they don't know anything. They don't know the drugs they're using, they don't know the side-effects of the drugs, they can't predict anything. So if you ever had a tendency to rely on the authority of doctors as a source of solace and security, that you're in good hands, at least in my kind of cancer it's not true."

Although we want and expect them to be experts, doctors sometimes *don't* have all the answers, which can be as frustrating for them as for us. For some illness or undiagnosed symptoms they may have few remedies, or even none at all. And even when medical science has general answers, each person is different and so there are still many unknowns. Doctors often can't predict how a given person will react to a particular disease or treatment. In some cases, making decisions is very much like gambling — which can be very frustrating for those who aren't gamblers.

As with any issue, there's sometimes another side to dependency. It can be welcomed as well as despised. For some people, illness lets them be more dependent than they would normally allow themselves to be. A hospital stay may be a vacation, a chance to get away from the chaos, demands, unpleasantness, or even dullness of home or work. It's a chance to be taken care of, to slow down and relax, to let go of the pressures and demands of everyday life. This isn't always bad. Illness may allow people who aren't able to slow down and relax in their everyday lives to do something when they're sick that they should do more often anyway.

In spite of the general feelings of powerlessness, sick people sometimes *do* have a lot of power. This power can be positive and help the healing process or it can be negative and hurt or hinder it. Not taking your medication; not following doctors orders about diet, rest, and exercise; and even your attitude — all these can affect your illness. That's power. When I asked a person with serious diabetes, "So whether you live or die really depends on you?," he replied:

"That's it — it's like being a god. The spark of life is in your hands. Just by how you live your life you can snuff yourself out. But with me it's more obvious."

This power to affect your illness can be a mixed blessing; it can allow you to feel more powerful and more involved in the healing process — but it can also be a tremendous burden and lead to guilt, as we'll see in Chapter 11.

HOW TO DEAL WITH POWERLESSNESS AND DEPENDENCY

Because helplessness and powerlessness arise in large part out of a loss of control, regaining some control over your illness and your life can lessen those feelings. To do that: 1) break down the task, 2) control your environment as much as possible, 3) improve physical limitations, 4) learn to understand and take control of your emotions, and 5) obtain information.

HOW TO DEAL WITH POWERLESSNESS

1. Break down the task into manageable parts.
2. Control your environment as much as possible.
3. Improve any physical limitations as much as possible.
4. Take control of your emotions, one by one, so you're not overwhelmed.
5. Obtain information: it leads to power.

---

1. BREAK DOWN THE TASK

A large task may seem (and be) overwhelming. But most can be broken down into small, more manageable parts. Rather than attempt to tackle everything at once, break it down and chip away.

Ask friends to help you; working together to solve problems will decrease your feelings of aloneness and being overwhelmed by it all — and increase your sense of power. More people working on a problem may also bring quicker results.

2. CONTROL YOUR ENVIRONMENT

Even when you're sick, there are ways to gain more control of your life. Although some may seem minor, don't underestimate them — anything that gives you a little more control may make you feel better.

Although it's difficult to control your environment if you're in the hospital, you can try. Perhaps you could hang favorite pictures on the wall, or wear a few items of your own clothing or jewelry. If you have a radio or tape deck, you can listen to your favorite music. You might ask friends to bring some of your favorite foods from outside (if they're acceptable to the hospital). To increase privacy at certain times, you could even try hanging a "do not disturb" or "please knock before entering" sign on the door.

You can exercise some control over your schedule and your visitors. If you have a phone, visitors could call beforehand to arrange convenient visiting times and find out what your needs are that day. Try to arrange the types of visits you'd prefer. Inviting friends to come in groups might create a more normal situation and take some of the focus off of you, if that's what you'd like. Inviting people to come one at a time might give you more chance to talk with each one. Or you can ask visitors to bring specific things for entertainment, such as cards or games, or invite them to come and watch a ball-game or a TV movie with you.

If you're taking medication you may be able, working with your doctor, to have some control over what drugs you take and when you take them, to better control pain or to minimize drowsiness or other side-effects. Adjusting medication so you are as alert as possible during doctors' visits can allow you greater participation in your care and give you not only a feeling of having some control but more *real* control as well.

This isn't an exhaustive list of ways to increase your control but if you understand that some of your feelings come from a lack of power and control, you may be able to find many other ways to increase your power. Every little bit helps.

3. IMPROVE PHYSICAL LIMITATIONS

There are tangible things you can do to lessen physical limitations and improve the quality of your life. Again, this is an area where friends can be helpful. You can make adjustments or adaptations in your home, such as add ramps, railings or handles, or remove carpets. You can buy or make tools or implements to help you do things more easily. Many mechanical aids exist to increase mobility and function. Someone whose hands are restricted by arthritis, for example, can obtain a variety of gadgets such as jar openers, special door knobs, and velcro closures; someone who can't speak may be able to use a computer that can speak. New aids are constantly being created, and although some are very technologically advanced and expensive, others are simple and easy to make. Be creative — see what you can make or find to meet your needs.

Ask your medical team, including doctors, nurses, physical therapists, and social workers, for their help in maximizing your mobility and function. They've had experience with this and may have good ideas. If drugs are impairing your function, talk to your doctor about that as well (see Chapter 14).

4. TAKE CONTROL OF YOUR EMOTIONS

By gaining more control over all the emotions discussed in this book, you'll be less ruled by them and more in control of your life.

5. OBTAIN INFORMATION

Information is a key to power. One of the best ways to regain some power over your life is to obtain as much information about your illness and the normal functioning of the human body as you can. (For more on finding information, see Chapter 2.)

FOR FRIENDS AND FAMILY

Friends and family can be very helpful in all these areas. Be creative. Help find ways for the person who's sick to get information; help them do as much as they want and can, thereby lessening their dependency; help them increase their mobility and function level; and help them gain more control over their illness and their life during this difficult time. But don't be so anxious to help that you help *too* much, thereby adding to the dependency.

DEPRESSION

"Just being in the hospital, being bedridden, being that dependent, I really got depressed. That became a real crisis. There didn't seem to be any end to it."

"Depression is terrible. I wake almost every single morning feeling like I really don't want to do it any more. If I have to live six more months like this I'm going to kill myself."

CAUSES OF DEPRESSION

Depression, sadness, and grief often accompany illness. They are natural reactions to loss — and illness causes many types of losses. Illness usually changes life as you knew it, so that even though you continue to eat and breathe, illness is sometimes seen as almost a form of death — and you may need to mourn the loss as you would a death.

"I'm losing my health, my job, my daughter...it's like a tragedy. I'm not dying, but in a way I feel like I am."

These are real losses, major losses, and certainly good reasons to feel depressed. But small things can also cause depression.

"It's depressing to see sunshine and not be mobile. I miss the gardening. It's the first time in my life I've had my own garden and I can't even use it." [from a woman with a badly broken leg]

Depression when you're sick is caused by very real factors. Understanding that and knowing that it's so common may at least give you one less "symptom" to worry about. Depression that comes with illness should be treated as routinely as postpartum depression after childbirth. Perhaps if the depression that accompanies illness had a special name such as "illness depression," we would recognize and deal with it more routinely.

Illness is simply a difficult time. That's normal. Bad news needs time to sink in; you need time to process and accept new information, and figure out how to respond to it. This may lead to a "period of darkness" that will in time go away naturally.

Depression can also be caused by various medications that are being used to treat other problems. This is an important reason to mention those feeling to your doctor, and ask if the depression might be caused by the medications.

 Sometimes depression is caused by inaccurate information. What if a person who is recovering, for example, thinks he's dying? What does that do to someone's will to live?

When my father was recovering from heart surgery, he seemed very depressed and just lay there without smiling when the doctor told him that his heart was doing fine. I was puzzled by this lack of reaction to what I thought was good news. Finally my father (who couldn't speak because he was on a respirator) made me understand that of course his heart was working well — with the pacemaker. Since his surgery was to replace a bad valve and not to install a pacemaker, he viewed that as a real defeat, a sign that his heart couldn't work alone. I asked the doctor about the pacemaker, and was told that an external one had been placed near his bed as a routine precaution but it wasn't hooked up! My father had assumed it was hooked up (there were so many tubes and wires attached to him) and that depressed him. When I finally understood the confusion and had the doctor explain the medical situation to my father, he felt much better.

Later, when my father was still on the respirator but getting better, the doctors switched him to a machine that was bigger and more complicated so he could breath as much as possible on his own. The machine would make up the difference, rather than doing all his breathing for him. But nobody bothered to explain this to him. He saw the bigger machine and assumed his condition had worsened. Again, when I got the doctor to explain the reason for the bigger machine, my father was reassured. Each time, however, I had to play detective to unravel the miscommunication.

Although some of my father's depression during this period was understandable, much of it was caused and/or accentuated by absurd (and avoidable) communications problems. Nobody at the hospital noticed or paid attention to his depression, much less searched for the causes.

SEVERE DEPRESSION: THE DEEP DARK PIT

Sometimes illness causes severe depression. I think of this kind of depression as similar to being at the bottom of a deep dark pit — a pit that appears too deep to be able to climb out of.

You can't see out and the sun never shines down inside. Your perspective is distorted because all you can see are the sheer sides of the pit and so it's hard to image that there's anything beyond it. There's a hopeless feeling because you can't see any way out — and you can't see anything outside that might inspire you to *want* to get out. Your eyes become so accustomed to the dark that you'd have trouble seeing in bright daylight. Your muscles become so weak from disuse after such a long time in the pit that they no longer function well. So why even try to find a way out?

HOW TO DEAL WITH DEPRESSION

What can you do if you're depressed? What can you do to help someone who's depressed about their illness? Depression is a complex problem but there are things that might help, including: 1) talking, 2) clarifying information, 3) increasing your power and control, 4) exercise, 5) doing enjoyable activities, and 6) seeking professional help if needed.

HOW TO DEAL WITH DEPRESSION

1. Talk — with friends, family, or professionals.
2. Clarify information and assumptions.
3. Increase your power and control.
4. Exercise.
5. Do things you enjoy.
6. Seek professional help when appropriate.

---

1. TALK

If you're depressed, it's often helpful just to talk, to express your feelings. You can talk with family, friends, or professionals (such as a psychologist or social worker). If there's no one you can talk to, try writing down your feelings. Keep a diary, journal, or write stories. You may later want to share those writings with someone — or you may not.

To continue my deep dark pit analogy, even if the person at the bottom can't see any light it's nevertheless important for friends and family standing next to the pit to be clear about what's outside — and to understand what it feels like to be down there at the bottom.

Friends can help by being good listeners. If someone you know is depressed because of their illness, you can listen, clarify reality, help the person obtain information, encourage them to do little things that may make them feel better, and help them get more control over their life and illness.

To simply say, "Cheer up, don't be sad, don't be depressed" may imply that there's no reason to be sad and depressed. It's seldom effective and may just make the person who's sick think you don't understand. To someone who has very real reasons to be unhappy, it can seem almost like an insult. This doesn't mean you can't try to lighten things up, but don't ignore the feelings of the person who's sick.

"The doctor said to me, 'You're too depressed, stop worrying, you're making yourself sicker.' He got me so angry. 'Stop worrying,' he said. After a year of being sick without any answers, how can I not worry."

2. CLARIFY INFORMATION AND ASSUMPTIONS

In addition to providing an outlet for those feelings, talking may clarify what the feelings really are and on what they're based. Sometimes depression is based on false assumptions. And how we cope with the depression, or help others to cope, may depend on the reality of the situation. There's a big difference between the person who has a simple infection that will eventually heal on its own and the person with diabetes and an infected foot who may face amputation because it isn't healing. There is also a great difference between the person with a broken leg who'll be out of the emergency room in an hour with a light walking cast and no pain, and the person with a serious break who'll have to remain in traction for three months, unable to get out of bed. But the person who's sick may not always be able to see the difference. That's part of the nature of depression.

3. INCREASE YOUR POWER AND CONTROL

Powerlessness is also a factor in depression.   Part of depression is a sense of powerlessness and helplessness — that there's nothing you can do about the bleak situation you see. So dealing with the powerlessness (see Chapter 5) may help the depression.

Little changes can make a big difference. One hospitalized young man who's leg was in traction and who had kept his curtains closed for several months told me:

"Why do I keep the curtains drawn?   Because it's too depressing to see the sunshine and be tied to this bed. I can't go out so I'd rather not see it."

After much persuasion I obtained permission from his doctor and head nurse to wheel his bed, traction and all, outside on the patio one afternoon. The next day his curtains were open and morale began improving.

Find positive things to do, no matter how small. Every little bit helps.

4. EXERCISE

Physical exercise may also help. The more scientists learn about the interconnections of the mind and body, the more they discover real physical reasons why exercise makes you feel better. Among other things, exercise releases endorphins, which are chemicals in the brain that act as natural painkillers and increase feelings of well-being.

5. FIND ACTIVITIES YOU ENJOY

Do things you enjoy or do well, whether it's playing the piano, gardening, bowling, or walking in the woods. These activities can provide a welcoming spot of light in an otherwise dark pit, even if you find you don't enjoy them as much as you normally might. If you can allow yourself to feel good sometimes, then the pit won't seem so dark.

Consider doing things to help others. That (and their gratitude) may help you feel needed and useful — and that you can make a difference.

6. SEEK PROFESSIONAL HELP

Although some depression is normal with illness, the depression can sometimes be severe or prolonged and can be difficult to deal with on your own. In those cases it's important to seek professional help.

There's a big difference between the normal feelings of sadness and grief related to illness, that will get better with time, and the hopelessness associated with a serious (clinical) depression. Serious depression doesn't necessarily diminish with time and may be out of proportion to the reality of the situation. Symptoms of clinical depression include: a change in your eating habits, such as poor appetite or overeating; a change in sleeping habits, such as insomnia or sleeping most of the time; low energy or fatigue; poor concentration or difficulty making decisions; and feelings of hopelessness.

Let your doctor know if you're feeling depressed and how much it's affecting you. If you're unsure whether you're feeling a temporary depression related to your illness or a clinical depression that should be treated, talk with your doctor about it. Your doctor can help you determine whether help for the depression itself might be appropriate and, if so, what kind. Psychologists and psychiatrists are experienced in helping people with depression.

Check whether any medication you're taking for your illness may be causing the depression — and adjust if necessary. Since depression involves bio-chemical changes in the body (as well as psychological attitude), medication can sometimes be very effective to counter it. Various forms of counselling can also be helpful. Again, discuss this with your doctor.

If you're a friend and you think someone you care about is depressed, talk to them about it. If they don't acknowledge it and you think it's interfering with the healing process, it may be appropriate to mention your concern to the doctor, working through the family member acting as liaison.

WORTHLESSNESS

"What do I have to feel good about myself right now? All the things that I used to take tremendous pride in — my job, parenting, my network of friends — they're no longer reliable. What do I have to feel good about? Very little. So that makes me feel bad about me."

"I feel so sick, so weak, so inhuman, so not myself."

"I used to dance, jog every day, ride a motorcycle. I'm not used to being inactive. It's not me."

"I had always been a very physical guy, had always had tremendous strength and endurance and a lot of energy. For the next year I was like a fragile egg."

Illness will affect your self-image and self-worth. It's very disorienting to feel different, not to be able to do the old familiar things, not to be able to trust your body to respond in the usual ways. All these changes affect your self-image and self-worth.

In our society we too often measure our worth as a person by external things — our job, financial standing, kids, physical appearance, clothes, cars, and/or athletic prowess. Our image of ourselves (as well as other people's image of us) depends a lot on these things. Since illness can affect all of these, it shouldn't be surprising that illness affects our self-image and our feelings of self-worth.

If illness itself makes you doubt your self-worth, the manner in which sick people are often treated will only fuel these feelings. Some friends don't know how to relate to someone who's sick and may keep their distance, or they may relate to you only as a "sick person" rather than as they used to. They may speak louder when you're in a wheelchair even though your hearing may be fine. They may treat you as less competent simply because your arm is in a cast. They may not discuss certain things because they think you are more emotionally fragile or because they feel they can't bother you with certain issues. And they may simply stay away because they don't feel comfortable with illness, hospitals, or some of the emotions you may be feeling.

To the medical establishment you may be just another patient — just another broken leg, or flu, or heart attack — with a case number and a set of vital statistics. Medical data about your illness becomes their primary concern — everything else is secondary. Your needs, values, personality, and accomplishments are all unimportant.

> *"I remember being taken down to X-ray. I was on the gurney and felt just like a side of beef. They roll you around and get you in the right position and bend your legs this way and that. That dehumanizing kind of feeling was really unpleasant."*

Needless to say, that doesn't promote feelings of self-worth.

SELF-IMAGE

Our self-image, our sense of identity, depends on many things. It's primarily based on our internal sense of who we are — a sense that we've developed from our perspectives and experiences over the years. But although self-image begins to be formed in early childhood, as an adult it's greatly influenced by four factors:

1) body image (the look and function of our body)
2) psychological make-up,
3) role and position in our family (in economic, social, and emotional terms)
4) role in society (our work and other social, religious, and/or political activities)

Illness can change many of these things, thereby altering our image of ourselves as well as other people's image of us.

1. BODY IMAGE

Since illness usually has a physical manifestation, our image of our body — how it looks and how it works — is very likely to be affected.

> *"When your body is hurting all the time you start to hate it."*

"I was a very active, athletic kid. I was on all the athletic teams and had a future of being an athlete and identified myself as being a jock. When I originally got the diabetes, I weighed 215 pounds; when I came out of the hospital I weighed 140. I'd lost everything, all my muscle tone. I looked like a walking skeleton."

"If you're on chemotherapy, there's a physical appearance of weirdness, of losing your hair and all that."

"I hate being a gimp, walking around with a limp. I've just not been feeling very attractive and happy about myself. You're only as pretty as you feel."

The changes in your body don't need to be major to have an impact. A sore arm from tennis elbow affected my self-image in ways I'm a little embarrassed to admit. I discovered that my strong right arm was a very important part of my self image. It was part of my independence and my sense of equality with males. I was very self-sufficient. I could do almost anything. I could throw a baseball and hammer nails better than most men. Then all of a sudden I couldn't do any of it.

Body image is complex: it doesn't always depend on the obvious. After my first mastectomy, I didn't think I was very concerned about my missing breast. I hadn't worried about that at all when I chose to have the mastectomy (where the whole breast is removed) rather than a less disfiguring lumpectomy (where only the tumor and some surrounding tissue is removed, leaving most of the breast). I never even considered reconstructive surgery. Although I've generally liked my appearance over the years, my self-image never depended on how my body looked.

As I looked in the mirror after the mastectomy, I saw exactly the same person as before. But at some point, a couple months after the surgery, I realized I wasn't feeling very good about my body and began to wonder if I was fooling myself and if I was really more concerned about the missing breast than I had admitted. I looked in the mirror again, and I realized I wasn't standing straight. The mastectomy, coupled with over-protection and insufficient arm exercises afterwards, had significantly weakened some arm and shoulder muscles and for a while the movement of my left arm was limited, which led to awkward posture and equally awkward movement.

All of a sudden I realized what was wrong. I wasn't graceful — and for me gracefulness has always been a key component of attractiveness. It had nothing to do with not having a breast; it was how I held my shoulders and how I moved. As soon as I realized this, I made an effort to pull my shoulders back and walk gracefully and not worry about protecting my left arm so much. The result was immediate. My body still had some healing to do and my arm had strength to regain, but I began to feel graceful again. I also increased my swimming exercises which helped my arm and shoulder regain strength and mobility more rapidly. My body image returned to normal.

Many things only indirectly connected to your illness can affect your body image. Gaining extra weight due to inactivity or medication or losing it because of your illness, or even not being able to wear your favorite clothes (because of a cast, brace, weight change, or hospital protocol) can make you see yourself differently. Even simple things like not being able to wash your hair or body properly, or not being able to have your hair cut or styled, can be important. After three days of being in the hospital following my mastectomy, the first thing I did after getting home was to get in the car to see if my arm worked well enough to drive. It did — and I drove immediately to get my hair cut and washed.

By looking closely and discovering exactly how the illness affects your physical self-image, you may discover things you can do to improve it. In any case, body image is not the only component of self-image.

2. PSYCHOLOGICAL IMAGE

Although body image is perhaps the first thing that comes to mind in terms of changed self-image due to illness, your psychological make-up can be equally affected.

"I felt really not myself. I had turned into something else, a sick person. And a sick person wasn't me. I didn't know how to cope with being a sick person. It was horrible."

"I suffered under the delusion that strong people don't get needy."

For some people strength and independence are key aspects of their self-image — and the dependency created by illness can be a great threat to that. Illness may make you aware of how dependent you really are on others, and you may lose faith in your ability to control your life. Be patient — your basic personality will re-emerge in spite of the illness.

But all the effects of illness aren't negative; coping successfully may bring out strengths you didn't know you had, thereby increasing your self-worth. Surviving an adversity such as illness can actually result in more self-confidence (see Chapter 12).

3. ROLE IN FAMILY

Individuals in families tend to fill certain roles, and interactions between family members often fall into patterns. These roles are often worked out slowly over a period of time, and the smooth functioning of the family or group depends on them — even though the existing system may not be fair or work all that well.

Some roles the members of a family assume relate to functions and divisions of labor (breadwinner, cook, nurse, money-manager, morale-booster, parent), and some deal with power and responsibility within the family (leader, follower, dependent).

Illness changes these roles and the balance between them in many ways.

"He feels real inadequate as a parent and he's had a lot of anger towards me since I've been sick because he feels that I've copped out on him and our daughter. He feels like he's had to take a major role and hasn't known how to do it."

"You can't earn a living. That's a very demeaning situation to be in."

Perhaps you can no longer provide for your family or even be self-supporting. Other members of the family (your wife, husband, children, or parents) may either have to go to work or contribute part of their hard-earned money so that you and your family can survive. That may alter your relationship with those people. Or suppose you receive disability or welfare benefits, with the limits and stigma often connected to that. What does it do to your self-image if you can't provide for yourself and your family as you did before or as you would like? Some people accept these changes easily, others don't.

What if you can't buy your children presents or new clothes for school? Suppose illness forces you to sell your house — or your car. Suppose you can't send your child away to college as you had planned, and she or he will have to go to the local community college or give up college altogether and work to support the family. Years of plans, hopes, and dreams down the drain. That may make you feel that you failed — as a parent, provider, or member of society.

Who will fill your role when you get sick? Will whoever fills the roles do it easily and well, or will it be difficult for them? If they do it well, will that usurp your role and make you feel even more useless? The discovery that others could fill your roles might be very threatening — or it could be liberating.

4. ROLE IN SOCIETY

Work can also be a source of pride, identity, and self-worth. Since we often categorize and judge people by the work that they do (paid or unpaid), changes in your ability to work will affect your identity.

"I meet people and they ask what I do. Well, I don't do anything these days except try to get well. It quickly ends the conversation."

For most people work is much more than just something to take up time or bring in money. For some it's the very purpose of life. How do you define who you are? How often do we simply answer by giving our occupation. "I am a printer, a teacher, an architect, a mother, a biologist, a writer." What if, all of a sudden, that changes — temporarily or perhaps permanently? You broke your arm and can't work for three months. You can't hold a hammer, drive a car, use a typewriter, or carry a child.

Sometimes the identity doesn't even depend on the particular job but on the type of work ("I'm a professional," "I'm a worker," or "I'm an executive") or even simply because you're employed ("I'm the bread-winner").

If you lose your job, will you think of yourself differently? Will others see you differently? Will they still like and respect you?

HOW TO DEAL WITH WORTHLESSNESS

Our self-image is based on past experience, but it can change. To increase your feelings of self-worth when you're sick, continue to do as many as possible of the old activities that gave you a sense of identity and worth. Then be creative and develop new activities to further increase your self-worth.

HOW TO DEAL WITH WORTHLESSNESS

1. Don't forget your real inner identity.
2. Continue old activities that gave you a sense of identity and self-worth:
     — pay attention to physical image (& exercise)
     — maintain your roles in the family & society.
3. Develop new activities that can build self-worth.

---

1. DON'T FORGET YOUR IDENTITY

Illness may change some things about you — but others will probably remain the same. As an exercise, make a list of words you would use to describe yourself (including body image, psychological image, and your role in your family and society). You might also make a second list of adjectives others would use to describe you. Then see how many of these things are affected by your illness. Do you still recognize yourself? How much has changed? Now go through the list again. Do all those things need to change? Are there areas you could make an effort to strengthen that would make you feel better about yourself? Or perhaps you'll look at the list and discover that although some things have changed, many haven't and you are still you.

2. CONTINUE YOUR OLD ACTIVITIES

In spite of your illness, maintain your sense of individual identity. Continue to do as many of the things that gave you this sense of self *before* your illness. Even though illness can occupy much of your time and thoughts, save time and energy to talk about and do the things that were important to you before. Ask your friends for their help. Tell them what you *can* do, as well as what you can't.

Looking as much like your old self as possible can help retain your sense of identity and self-worth. Being sick usually doesn't mean you can't wear clothes you like or style your hair.

"I always put on full make-up. That was a good hour ordeal — washing, putting on make-up, combing my hair." [this woman also wore her own bathrobe and favorite jewelry in the hospital]

Do whatever exercise you can — it will help your body feel good and that in turn will help you feel good. Even if you're flat on your back in a hospital bed, ask your nurse, doctor, or physical therapist about exercises you could do. If you've gained or lost weight, consider buying a few attractive new clothes.

If you can, read an engrossing book, walk through a park, visit a museum, or see a movie. Enjoy life as much as you can. Maintain your role in the family as much as you want and is possible.

3. DEVELOP NEW ACTIVITIES

Illness may also give you the time to try new activities you weren't interested in or didn't have time for before, some of which might give you pleasure and build self-esteem. Are there interesting hobbies you've never had the time to try before? Ask friends to suggest things they think you might like. Could some of these areas even lead to a future job or career?

You may also want to consider doing specific things that might help you feel good about yourself, such as helping a hospital roommate or a friend, exercising, writing a letter to someone in need, making a present for someone you care about, or simply writing or creating something beautiful. Helping others will almost always make you feel better about yourself. Above all, as surface things change, try to remember that it's who you are underneath that is really important.

All these challenges to your old self-image may lead you to re-examine the basis for that image — and re-evaluate what is (or should be) really important about yourself, people, and life in general.

FEAR

"I sometimes wake up in the middle of the night, or in the morning feeling an incredible terror. I'm trembling inside and trembling outside. It's sheer and utter terror, almost disbelief: how can this be happening to me. But it is." [from a woman with an undiagnosed illness that left her feeling very weak]

"Here I had a disease I'd never heard of, didn't understand at all, and hurt like a son of a bitch. It scared me to death." [from a woman with pericarditis, an inflammation of the heart lining]

The fear can be a distant uneasiness that something might happen at some future time, or it can be an immediate terrifying panic. Panic can come from the overwhelming immensity of the illness; the suddenness of it; the onset of a new, unknown or severe symptom; or from the intensity of the pain.

"I once thought I was dead, or on the edge of it. It later turned out to be diagnosed as a kidney stone. I was in a mountain cabin in Norway, totally cut off from everything, no phones, nothing, and I woke up one morning paralyzed, not totally physically paralyzed but virtually incapacitated, having no idea what was wrong with me. My wife then climbed down the mountainside with a map and as far as I knew she was gone forever and I was up there in this cabin and that was it."

Fears aren't any more rational than other emotions. You may not be in danger of dying, for example, and yet be very afraid of death. Similarly, a cold or sprained ankle may touch off a depression that seems to the outside observer to be way out of proportion for such a simple illness. One man I interviewed, who happened to be a doctor, told of his intense irrational fears when he received a simple cut.

"It was on my right hand and I was a surgeon and I thought of what would happen if I lost my finger or had some disability. I started to think, 'What if I get a brain abscess or endocarditis?' All these things are slightly implausible, but possible."

The fear touched off by illness can be of almost anything. It can include fear of: 1) death, 2) pain, 3) loss of limb or function, 4) abandonment, 5) recurrence, 6) contagion, 7) the unknown, or 8) a host of secondary worries.

1. FEAR OF DEATH

"There were moments early on, in my early twenties, when I had panic city, times when I would think my kidneys were going out and I was dying."

"I was scared to death. First of all it hurt so damn much. I couldn't believe that anything could hurt that much and not be dangerous. How can this hurt so much and I not die?"

Death may be a real possibility with some illnesses — even a certainty with others. And, of course, it's a certainty for all of us at some point. But death is seldom easy for us to deal with, especially the first few times we encounter it.

We expect this fear of death with serious illness, but it can also come when the illness is neither life-threatening nor even serious. Fears aren't necessarily rational. Illness may touch off fears of death simply because death is something that we all think about at times. Any illness can make us aware of our mortality.

"The business about being ill is that your body is breaking down, and that it's finally going to break down. That's what it's all about — your own mortality."

Most of us have some fear of death. That fear can be touched off by your own illness, the death or illness of a friend or relative, or a newspaper or television story about someone's death. It's no more "wrong" to think about death when you have a minor illness than when a friend has died. In fact, it's quite natural.

Not everyone fears death; some simply accept it as a part of life. For some it's actually a welcome relief — either from pain or from a slow decline toward death. Some are less afraid of death than of incapacitation and dependence and some even prefer to end their lives at a time of their own choosing, while they're still in control (see Chapter 15).

2. FEAR OF PAIN

"The other big worry is not so much dying as going through a long painful and emotionally trying decline. That's always been my biggest fear. If I was going to die, just close my eyes and die, that's fine. But just getting sicker and sicker, and in greater and greater pain, and more and more invalid...."

There are different kinds of fear of pain. There's an abstract theoretical fear of pain at some time in the future — and there's also a very immediate fear of upcoming pain when you have an illness that hurts a lot.

Although pain is subjective and we all perceive it differently, the degree of pain you feel will probably influence your level of fear.

Interestingly, one component of pain is actually *fear* of pain, especially when you don't have the power to control it. One method of pain management (originally used in hospices for dying patients but now also being used widely for pain in general) is to give pain medication before the last medication wears off and the pain begins to be felt. Thus medication is given on a regular schedule, tailored to your needs, rather than waiting until you begin to feel pain and request more medication. Another method, called patient controlled analgesia (PCA), gives you control, with limits, over a small pump that releases pain medication directly into an IV (intravenous) line, thus bringing almost immediate relief when you need it. Using these systems, doctors are often able to keep patients free of pain on lower doses than they would need if they waited until the pain was felt again. If either of these methods seems appropriate for you, discuss it with your doctor. (For more on pain, see Chapter 14.)

Another variation on the fear of pain is avoiding doing anything that you know will, or even might, cause pain. For example, you may avoid using a recently injured arm although it no longer actually hurts and there's no need to favor it. Family and friends may also avoid touching you, for fear of inadvertently hurting you. That's very considerate if you are sore — but you may not be.

After my mastectomy, friends were often a little awkward when they hugged me, perhaps fearful of hurting a sore area (although it had healed quickly). I was tempted to put one of those squeaky toys in my bra, next to the prosthesis, so that it would squeak when someone hugged me. That was my response to being treated like a china doll when I felt pretty normal. I never did it, although I did look unsuccessfully in a few toy stores. But I did the next best thing, which was to mention my idea to a few friends and that itself broke the ice. The hugs returned to normal.

3. FEAR OF LOSS OF LIMB OR FUNCTION

"The doctor said I'd keep losing my sight until I was totally blind, He didn't know how long that would take, but he was sure it would happen. "

"When my hip wore out, they told me I'd never walk again."

"I had a lot of fear about my feet because I didn't know if I was going to be crippled. For a while I had to wear awfully ugly orthopedic shoes. I was a teenager and I thought I wouldn't be popular with the boys. I couldn't dance. That scared me a lot."

"I thought maybe I'd messed myself up and couldn't have kids."

"I had a lot of concern about my sex drive. I didn't think I would die, but I thought I was ruined sexually." [from a man who got an infection after routine prostate surgery and required a temporary catheter for a short period.]

Death is a loss, the loss of life — but illness can also involve other losses which, although not as final, are important losses nevertheless. And precisely because you *won't* die, because you will be around to experience the losses, they may even have a greater impact than the loss of your life. These losses can include any loss of body function or appearance, loss of mobility, and loss of clarity of mind. These, in turn, can affect employment, life style, or even dreams and fantasies.

The first few weeks after my first mastectomy, I was very self-conscious about the loss of a breast — because there was a definite weight imbalance, because the area was still sensitive due to the healing process, and because that's what everyone else seemed to focus on. That lessened with time and after a while I seldom thought about the missing breast at all. Early on, a friend helped me put my mastectomy in perspective. Years ago, when I taught school, I had a five-year-old student who lacked an arm as a result of Thalidomide, a drug his mother had taken during her pregnancy. Steve never seemed to be bothered by his fake arm, nor did it stop him from doing what other kids did. His first day at school, when the other students stared at his plastic and metal prosthesis, Steve took it off, passed it around, and showed them how it worked — all very matter of factly. And that was that. The kids were curious but from then on, no one seemed to be very bothered by his arm.

Until I thought about Steve, most of my self consciousness about the mastectomy had been concern about not making other people uncomfortable. Then I realized that I never expected Steve to go through life wondering about whether his false arm made anyone *else* uncomfortable. That seemed absurd. In fact, his acceptance of his arm seemed to make others feel more at ease. I realized that I could adopt the same approach with my false breast. The next day when I began swimming at the local pool, I changed in the locker room without any of the discomfort I had previously assumed I'd feel. And I made another interesting discovery. My bathing suit, which easily hid the mastectomy, was not at all as successful at hiding the few extra pounds I was so self-conscious about on my hips and thighs. That bothered me more than the mastectomy — and I instinctively tied my towel around my waist, not my shoulders, as I went out to the pool!

A few weeks after the mastectomy, I had another learning experience. I had gone to Los Angeles for a conference and was staying with a friend. As soon as I put down my travel bag, she said, "Can I see your scar?" I hadn't expected the question and never thought that friends might be curious. But after all, we're told that one woman in eight (it was one in eleven when I began this book!) will get breast cancer. It will probably affect most of us, or a close friend or family member, at some point in our lives. Her honest curiosity helped me realize that, instead of being scared or threatened by breast cancer, people might be curious and welcome the chance to learn more about it.

Later, while visiting relatives in France, I felt a little awkward walking around in a bathrobe without my prosthesis — until I went into the bathroom and saw my cousin's teeth sitting in a glass. None of us is perfect — we're just more aware of our own imperfections.

How we picture our body is seldom objective, so it follows that how we see imperfections and losses will vary. For one person, the fear of retaining a small scar might be as great as someone else's fear of losing a leg. Objectively the small scar is minor by comparison, but it may not be minor to the person who has it. Fears, and body image, are not rational. I was much more concerned about the potential loss of function in my right arm from tennis elbow than I was about the loss of a breast from cancer. That made total sense to me — I use my right arm much more than my left breast. I depend on it for work and it's crucial for my independence.

Physical limitations not only affect your ability to perform everyday tasks, they also affect work and social life. Even minor restrictions that you can easily compensate for in your own home, such as not walking up stairs, not eating certain foods, or not opening heavy doors, become bigger problems in the outside world which is set up for the strong and healthy. Not only are you unable to do certain things, but the physical limitations constantly remind you, and others, that you're different, that you're sick.

A physical loss doesn't have to be specific — it can be as vague as the loss of good health. This is often a huge loss for someone facing their first major illness. If this occurs when we're beginning to feel middle-aged, we may fear that it's "the beginning of the end." When we're young we think that we're invulnerable. When illness strikes, we're shocked to discover that our body, which had always served us well and never caused trouble in the past, is neither perfect nor everlasting. Although there is much we can do to keep our bodies and minds strong and healthy, at some point the cells that for many years had been growing and getting stronger do begin an inevitable slow decline. We sometimes panic at the first sign, or what we perceive to be the first sign, of that process.

FEAR OF DEMENTIA

Fear of dementia or the loss of clarity of mind is especially common among older people, who are all too aware that such a loss may come at some point down the road. Media publicity about the tragedy of Alzheimer's Disease and other forms of dementia only accentuates those fears. An early sign of forgetfulness or mental fuzziness, whatever its cause or validity, may create panic.

Although some illnesses do affect clarity of mind, more often the symptoms are caused by medication. Some drugs can make you drowsy, confused, or unable to concentrate. Anxiety, caused by life in general or aggravated by the illness, can also lead to forgetfulness or disorientation, as well as to other physical symptoms. How do you know for sure that your symptoms are caused by drugs or anxiety and not by something more serious? What if it's a brain tumor, or Alzheimer's Disease? What's happening? Will the mental clarity ever return? Is it "the beginning of the end?" If you have these fears, talk to your doctor. He or she can determine the likely cause of those symptoms, adjust medication if necessary, and reassure you if your fears are unfounded.

4. FEAR OF ABANDONMENT

Fear of abandonment is sometimes a real and understandable part of illness.

"I'm afraid he'll leave, that if I'm sick for a long time he just won't be able to handle it and will leave. I try not to think about that much but it's always there."

"I'm losing my daughter. I asked her father to take her for a while and that's where she is at the present time... and it looks like she's going to be with him until I start feeling better."

"We'd planned a vacation, the second one we'd planned, and we couldn't go because I was feeling too ill. He kind of freaked out. He had gotten days off from work. I worry that if I'm sick for six more months or a year, the relationship won't last. That's very frightening to me."

"You worry about being abandoned by the people you love, you worry about the future, you worry about losing your support system, your social surroundings, the sources of your own ego gratification, about losing who the hell you are."

Illness can strain relationships with friends and family — and sometimes the sick person really does lose friends and lovers as a result. But real or not, the fear may be very strong.

A support network for and among friends can be important here. When some friends pull away due to fatigue or burnout, awareness on the part of both patient and friends that this can happen may help you prevent it. When one person needs time off due to burnout or simply because of life's other demands, perhaps others can fill the gap.

Some people worry about being abandoned by their doctors if their illness is serious or if the doctor has little to offer. One eighty-year old woman talked about her future:

"Doctor's aren't enthusiastic about taking care of the aged. Our diseases aren't very exciting, we aren't going to get much better, and some of us are going to die fairly soon — and they don't like that at all."

5. FEAR OF RECURRENCE

Some diseases do recur, while others might recur. You may still have the illness but it may be in remission. You may be completely cured but know you have a weak heart or weak knees that might succumb again. Or you may not know, for example, whether some stray cancer cells remained inside, ready to attack again.

> *"I can't get a pain anywhere now without worrying if it's come back."* [from a woman with breast cancer]

Some fears can continue long after the illness itself has been cured. The person who pulled a leg muscle may live with a constant fear of re-injuring it and may always slightly favor that leg. The person who sustained a broken leg in a car accident may be left with a fear of cars. These fears may be real or exaggerated, but they can greatly affect your life and how you live it.

> *"I'm very cautious now. I don't want to go back to the hospital. I'm even hesitant to do things like sports."*

> *"If I put my foot down the wrong way walking down the street, I might re-injure it. That's a constant fear. It makes me cautious in ways that I don't even know about."*

6. FEAR OF CONTAGION

Fear of contagion, of spreading the disease to others can be another concern. Friends and family sometimes fear "catching" the disease. This fear is obviously justified when the illness is contagious (spread by direct or indirect contact) or hereditary (passed on genetically to some or all of one's children) — but the fear may be present even when the illness isn't communicable. A man with a kidney condition which he rationally knew was not hereditary was still concerned.

> *"I wondered if in some way it contributed to my daughter's mental retardation, or if the other kids might get it."*

Friends may stay away out of fear of "catching" what you have, even if what you have isn't at all contagious. Some people even fear they can "catch" cancer or pass it on to someone else, which isn't true.

Fear of contagion may also be greatly exaggerated, as we've seen with AIDS, which can only be spread by certain very specific and limited kinds of contact. (I don't want to minimize the legitimate fear of catching or spreading AIDS through the ways that it can be spread — but there has been a tremendous amount of panic about catching AIDS from ways that it *can't* be spread.)

If you're already sick, pregnant, or taking immunosuppressant drugs as part of your treatment, you may fear catching another person's illness because you're more susceptible.

If you're worried about contagion, ask your doctor for more information or reassurance. In cases where contagion is a real possibility, your doctor can give you clear guidelines to prevent or minimize it.

7. FEAR OF THE UNKNOWN

You may also simply be afraid of the unknown. Some illnesses are very predictable, self-limiting, or easily treatable. Your body's immune system will eventually create antibodies and overcome a cold on its own in about 7-10 days. A cut will form a scab and heal in about a week. But other diseases are more complicated. As miraculous as modern medicine is, there are still many things that doctors don't know. They may not be able to find the cause of your symptoms, or if they find the cause, they may not have a cure. Doctors may generally know how to treat an illness but they may not be certain how your body will respond to that treatment. So prognoses, as well as causes and treatment, may be unknown — with the result that you, and the doctors, simply experiment — and hope. Meanwhile, your fears can run rampant.

"I'm scared because I don't know what my prognosis is. I don't know what I really have. I just know that I'm sick."

"The worst part is not knowing when the pain is going to end, not knowing what it is..."

But, as this person continued, there's also:

"the fear of knowing what it is, in case it turns out to be something terminal or chronic."

Even if much is known about your illness, *you* may not know it. When you're first diagnosed with an illness, you may not know anything about it's effects, prognosis, or remedies. Perhaps your doctor made a diagnosis but didn't have sufficient time to explain to you what that meant (or he or she didn't know and referred you to a specialist or you didn't have time to ask all you wanted to know). A thousand questions may come to mind — but there is no one to answer them right then. Perhaps you even have another appointment to find out more — but it's days, or weeks, away. Until your questions are answered, you're facing the unknown.

When the cause and course of your illness are known, you can at least make plans. With the unknown, it's more difficult. You know some things in your life will change, but you don't know exactly what, how, and for how long. It's hard to take control of the unknown — but you can try to obtain more information as quickly as possible.

8. SECONDARY WORRIES

As if the illness itself isn't enough to worry about, people will often be concerned about money, their families, or work. Because illness can be so expensive, many fears involve very practical concerns.

"There's always anxiety about the hospital bill. I keep telling myself that if I can relax about this I'll get well quicker and the bill won't be as big. But I can't relax because we just don't have the money for me to be sick."

"You worry about money. Very concretely, how will you make a living, could you get a job, how would you survive on the pittance they give us on disability. You fantasize about being sick and old in one of those flea-trap downtown hotels."

"I had friends to pick up the pieces of my life but I see people whose lives are literally going to be devastated by being in the hospital: women who were going to lose their jobs so there would be nothing to go back to and who can't pay the rent. You'd better have friends before you get sick, because if you don't you're really up the creek."

How will the family survive financially if you were the sole or primary breadwinner? Who will provide emotional support if you were the main source of strength or comfort? Who will fill the various roles you played if you're unable to fill them for some time, or permanently? Instead of marshalling your limited energy to deal with the illness at hand, you may be worrying about all these other things.

Work can also be a big source of worries. A man who had just begun his own business worried that it might collapse while he was in the hospital, and spent hours on the phone with his relatives who were managing the business in his absence. All he could think about was his hamburger shop. The medical staff thought those concerns were minor compared to the very serious medical problems he faced. They didn't realize how important it was to him to have finally realized his lifelong dream of owning his own business. Perhaps worrying about the business also served another purpose for him: perhaps it temporarily took his mind off his injuries and the big medical problems he would eventually have to face.

You may worry about a million little things. One woman who was in the hospital called her teenage daughter every morning to check on what clothes the daughter was wearing to school and whether they were well-matched and ironed. She wanted to make sure her daughter continued to look good. She was trying her best to maintain her role as a parent. Another mother constantly worried about her son's grades and school attendance. Everybody has their own particular set of concerns.

> *"Suddenly I'd remember that someone must call the Boy Scouts and tell them that I couldn't be a den mother and have them at my house next Friday."*

> *"There weren't going to be any clean clothes unless somebody took care of them."*

There are so many worries for a parent in normal times — and there are bound to be even more if you're sick.

Some worries are silly and far-fetched. After my first mastectomy I had a new false breast — a silicone prosthesis that fit into my bra and cost over $150. I worried about how fragile it was and how much it would cost to replace if it were damaged. The surgery had devastated my finances and the thought of any extra expense was scary. I love cats, but I was afraid a cat might accidentally puncture the prosthesis with its claws so I avoided picking up cats (including my own) for several months. Silly, but true.

In addition, because the surgeon had removed some of the lymph nodes under my arm, my lymph system was less able to handle what would normally be simple infections and I was therefore warned to avoid getting any cuts or scratches on my left arm. A couple weeks later I heard about a woman who developed a severe infection from a dog bite because of her weakened lymph system. I began to worry about any dog I passed on the street. I would discretely put my hand in my pocket or casually hold it up out of reach until I was safely past the dog. I tried to be inconspicuous about this since at the time I was embarrassed to reveal my fear to all but close friends — nor did I want the dog to know I was afraid. As time went on, I inevitably got scratches and none became infected so I relaxed and went back to petting the neighborhood dogs and cats.

HOW TO DEAL WITH FEAR

What should you do about all these fears? As I've already mentioned, one of the best first steps in dealing with fear (and other emotions) is to share your feelings. Talking is almost always useful. Just expressing your feelings out loud and sharing them with friends may begin to diffuse them. It may also help you to clarify your fears, get information, and gain more power and control.

HOW TO DEAL WITH FEAR

1. Identify the fear.

2. Keep an open mind

3. Obtain accurate information.

4. Increase your power and control.

5. Take positive actions to prevent
    or minimize problems.

---

1. IDENTIFY THE FEAR

A good beginning step in dealing with fear is to find out, as precisely as you can, what the fear is. If you're afraid of death, what exactly is the fear? Do you fear the end of life? Are you afraid of what will happen afterwards, possible pain before death, leaving loved ones alone, leaving work unfinished? Once you know exactly what you're afraid of, there may be things you can do to address that particular issue.

It's easy to make incorrect assumptions about another person's fear. When I worked in a large city hospital, I met two people whose fears had not been calmed by staff because no one had discovered what the real fear was and so all staff efforts to deal with it were aimed in the wrong direction.

Carlos, age 8, cringed in fear whenever the doctor approached to change the dressing on an ugly burn on his leg. The doctor assumed Carlos was afraid of pain and reassured him that the dressing change wouldn't hurt. He then insisted on simply getting on with the job in spite of Carlos' protests. When I *asked* Carlos about his fear, I learned it was not of pain but of how the burn, which included a skin graft, would look. Changing the dressing exposed the wound and the ugliness scared him. When I learned what the real fear was, I brought the doctor back and he talked to Carlos about the skin graft and the healing process. He explained what the area would look like when it was completely healed and why it looked so strange in the meantime. That information didn't change how the burn looked, but it did ease Carlos' fears about the future and even made him a little curious to watch the magical healing process. From then on, dressing changes were no longer traumatic events.

Alex, age 40, had a very serious leg injury resulting from a car accident, which would affect his ability to walk and to work. Although the doctors were trying hard to save his legs it seemed likely that he would lose part of one or both of them. Trying to be sensitive to his fears, his family and the hospital staff spent much time trying to reassure him about his future ability to get around and hold a job. They carefully explained how well prostheses could work. But no one knew, because no one asked, that his major fear was that no woman would find him attractive with an amputated leg. He thought he'd never find a wife and would have to spend the rest of his life alone. Once we discovered his real fear, we were able to address it.

It's important to differentiate between fears that are based on medical facts and those that are unfounded. It's important to know, for example, whether you're dealing with the real possibility of death or an abstract fear of it. That doesn't mean the ungrounded fears are any less "real" or less valid. If you want to talk about your fear of dying, go ahead. Be sure you're clear about the facts of your illness — but whatever the facts, it's still OK to *think* about death, and *talk* about it.

If death is a real possibility you'll probably deal with the fear differently, and in addition you'll have to deal with the reality of the upcoming death itself (see Chapter 15).

2. KEEP AN OPEN MIND

Your fears may not come true. Be open to the possibility that your fears may not happen. That may be little consolation, and it may not take away the fear, but at least try to be open to that possibility.

3. OBTAIN INFORMATION

Since information can be a source of power, the more you know about your illness (and good health and your body in general), the more you'll be able to participate in decisions and treatment. (For more on obtaining information, see Chapter 2.)

Getting sufficient, clear, and accurate information is important in dealing with fear. It can both help to determine how realistic the fear is and also help calm you if the fear is unfounded. The word cancer, for example, often conjures up images of death, which frightens people. But in reality, many types of cancer are now curable, if caught early. Although statistics on survival rates for various diseases have their limits, they can also sometimes be very reassuring.

Most pain can now be controlled, and understanding how and how well that can work for you may ease your fear of pain.

If the fear is of the unknown, you can obtain more information, as well as explore what different possibilities might be. Talking can sometimes help make the unknown more familiar. The more you talk, the more familiar you may become with the illness and with all the new information about it. This may lessen the fear.

If your fear is based on incorrect information or assumptions, accurate information may help.

If the fears are based on reality, obtaining clear and correct information allows you to go on to deal with the implications of that information. Is death a real possibility? How likely? How soon? What will the intervening time be like? What help and resources are available? Is some kind of disability a real possibility? What kind? What will that mean in terms of function and/or appearance? What changes will it mean for your life? What help is available? What are the options? This won't make the problem go away, but you've taken the first step. You can then go on, whether that means mourning the loss or finding ways to deal with it in the best way possible.

As we discussed earlier, another person — friend, family, or hospital staff member — can often be of great assistance in helping to obtain information.

4. INCREASE YOUR POWER AND CONTROL

Fears are often related to the issues of power and control. We're often less afraid when we have more control over our lives. So gaining more control over both your environment and your emotions may decrease some fears (see Chapter 5).

5. TAKE POSITIVE ACTIONS

Identifying your fears and obtaining accurate information may let you discover that, instead of simply focusing on the fears, there may be specific constructive actions that both you and your friends can take right away to help minimize or prevent problems.

Exercise or physical therapy might be effective to remedy a specific problem, to regain strength in general, to help boost the immune system, or just for morale. Remember that exercise releases endorphins that decrease pain and increase your sense of well-being.

Different fears call for different steps — many of which will become obvious when you identify the exact fear. Adapting furniture or arranging for transportation or physical therapy can lessen the impact of loss of mobility or function.

For fear of pain, perhaps the doctors and nurses can be extra careful to avoid pain as much as possible and can tell you ahead of time what to expect with each procedure. Sometimes you can be given choices about the procedure or pain medication, thus giving you more control over the situation. This may seem obvious, but unfortunately it doesn't always happen. Sometimes the convenience of doctors and nurses takes priority over your needs. Sometimes the medical staff assumes you know more than you do (or that you've already received the information from another staff member). And sometimes there just doesn't seem to be enough time for the staff to do everything that "should" be done to minimize pain. Extra interest and awareness by you or your friends or family can often make a difference. Sometimes the medical staff will need to be reminded or prodded — so remind them and prod them. Ask for what you need. Ask politely; but ask loudly and clearly.

Some techniques, such as relaxation and self-hypnosis, can help control pain and fears. Some of these techniques may be obvious, but others — such as breath control to ease labor pains — aren't natural and have to be learned and practiced. Learning the techniques won't solve all your problems, but it is something positive that can often be extremely helpful. Friends and family can help with relaxation exercises and many books include sample relaxation techniques (see Kabat-Zinn, *Full Catastrophe Living*, and Benson, *The Relaxation Response*).

Relaxation and exercise are valuable even when you're not sick. Fear, like guilt, can motivate you to do a variety of things that are good for you.

Even unfounded fears of death may prompt us to do things that are good to do anyway. As a therapist, I participated in a staff training workshop where we were all asked what we would do if we were told we only had a year to live. It helped us think about what we really wanted to do with our lives, and what we wanted to say to people. At the end of the workshop we realized the obvious — that we didn't have to wait until we were dying to do those things. That's a good exercise for anyone to do, at any time.

Worries about families and work can often be eased by knowing that other people can take (or are already taking) at least partial responsibility for those concerns. Tell others about your worries and let them help you resolve them. They may not do things exactly as you would — but the important thing is that they get done.

LONELINESS

"It's real lonely. It's the loneliest I've ever been, even with all those people around I just felt completely alone. No words could ever describe how I felt."

"It creates a sense of isolation, especially during the day because my friends are at work, so I spend more time by myself."

Illness can lead to loneliness, isolation, and boredom. This may be especially true if you're in a hospital, if you don't have many friends or family members around, or if your illness keeps you confined. And perhaps you don't feel very communicative when people are around — which can lead to an even greater feeling of isolation. You may be with people physically but without enough energy to relate to them in the way you'd like.

When you're alone and don't need anything, you may be aware of the aloneness and perhaps sad about it. But when you need something and there is no one there, the aloneness may take on a desperate quality.

"I was alone in the house, Not only would my cries for help not be heard, but I couldn't even make any. I might as well have been in the Sahara dying of thirst." [from a woman in bed for a few days with a bad flu!]

Some people have a difficult time being alone even when they are well — and illness only makes it more difficult.

"I'm living alone now, and that's hard. But who'd want to live with me here like this?"

"It's frightening to be sick and alone. I've been waking up a lot in the middle of the night, sick, and I've been by myself and it's really hard."

"I just wanted someone around."

Days in bed can go by slowly. Little things like having a radio, television, or a phone within reach can make a huge difference. If you're not well enough to read or do things, or if medication is affecting your vision, there may be nothing to do but sit, or lie, in bed. Or worse. Imagine spending weeks (or months) lying on your back with a leg in traction, unable to get out of bed, or with a jaw wired shut so that you can't really talk or eat regular food. You may be on a respirator or in an intensive care ward. Perhaps you're not experiencing anything that dramatic, but you just don't have much energy — and the time passes so very slowly. Perhaps you're totally alert but have to rest quietly to let your body heal. Or you may feel totally fine but can't get around well enough to do the things that you would normally do.

"It gets real boring! I've started more needlework projects and crossword puzzles, all of which are things I wouldn't normally do. What can you do in bed? There are only so many things you can do, and especially because I couldn't focus enough to read or write. It was utterly boring. There are only so many

conversations you can have, only so many hours you can have visitors. And only so many hours of visitors you can take."

"The hardest part was lying on my back all day, without doing anything. I mean, I couldn't do anything at all. I couldn't even move."

The impersonality of the hospital can cause emotional isolation.

"I have not been touched, really touched, by more than two members of this hospital staff though I've been handled by 30 or more already in the last few days. The touch, the human touch, means so much."

For some people the aloneness has another dimension: it forces them to realize just how alone in the world they really are.

"I've battled this mostly by myself. I haven't had anybody to take care of me."

"I have lots of acquaintances — but I discovered that I have no friends. No one, not one, has come here to visit me."

It's amazing how many people in hospitals have no visitors. Some people have casual acquaintances but no real friends — and their acquaintances may not even notice the sick person's absence. Even if you have friends or family, they may live too far away to visit, or to visit often. Or they themselves may be too old or sick to come and visit you; or they may have too many other responsibilities, such as work or young children to care for. Some friends may also be scared away by illness.

> *"A friend stopped by and then she didn't call me for a month. When she called, she said, 'I'm going to be perfectly straight — you looked so bad and you'd lost so much weight that I was terrified and I just couldn't relate.' Other people just kind of fade out but don't acknowledge what they're doing."*

Perhaps you do have visitors, but no one with whom you can really talk openly and honestly about what's really bothering you — what you're thinking or worrying about. That's a whole other kind of loneliness — one that can exist even with many people around.

> *"It's lonely because people don't understand. They don't know what it's like."*

Although loneliness is unbearable for many who are sick, for some people there is another side to it. Aloneness is not necessarily lonely. Aloneness may be a welcome change from a hectic life. It may be a chance to reflect and evaluate various aspects of your life, it may let you rest peacefully or do things you don't normally have a chance to do. It may get you away from the constant commotion of life and all the people you're normally with. All of this may be welcome and even beneficial. This chance for reflection and evaluation was often mentioned by people when I asked about the good aspects of being sick (see Chapter 12).

HOW TO DEAL WITH LONELINESS

Aloneness, isolation, and boredom are feelings you can often do something concrete about — by getting help from old and new friends and finding specific activities to occupy your time. This probably won't just happen automatically, however.

HOW TO DEAL WITH LONELINESS

1. Mobilize your friends: tell them you need them — and what you need.
2. Make new friends; reach out to help others.
3. Find activities, old or new, to occupy your time.

---

1. MOBILIZE YOUR FRIENDS

If friends ask what you need when you're sick, tell them if you'd like some company — and what times are best for you and what kind of companionship you'd like. Do you want one visitor at a time (to be able to talk more intimately), or would you like several (so you might fit into a group conversation more naturally or so you wouldn't have to work so hard to uphold your end of a conversation)? Do you want friends to come over to talk, to watch something special on TV with you, play cards, read to you, entertain you, help you do things, or simply to sit quietly with you or be nearby doing their own thing but not necessarily talking with you? Do you want hugs? Do you want to just let out your feelings or cry? Let your friends and family know.

If you feel alone because others don't understand what it's like to be sick, maybe you can help. Visitors aren't mind readers so they may understand you better if you share more of your feelings. I hope that this book will help bridge this communication gap — by providing clues to possible feelings and by urging both those who are sick and their friends and family to talk about those feelings.

If you're seriously ill and haven't told a lot of friends, do it now. Expand your friendship circle. Think of people outside your inner group who would want to know you're sick and who might be supportive. Now is not the time to be shy. If you have a hard time doing this, ask friends to help. If you have a hard time calling people, write a letter.

If you're already visiting someone who is lonely and wants company, call other friends and urge them to visit also, perhaps even suggesting times and offering hints about what the sick person might need. Too often friends are afraid they'll be in the way — or won't know how to act or what to say.

2. MAKE NEW FRIENDS

Reach out to other people who may be lonely. If you're in the hospital, the staff may be able to help you find other patients who'd like companionship. If you're not in the hospital, involve yourself in group activities. Develop new interests if your old ones don't keep you busy or bring you in contact with people. Don't forget support groups for your illness — they can lead to new friendships.

Helping others will not only decrease boredom; it can also earn you much appreciation and make you feel better about yourself. If you're confined to your house, explore ways you can help others by phone. Check with your local volunteer bureau.

3. FIND ACTIVITIES TO OCCUPY YOUR TIME

You may have much more free time when you're sick — but you may not be able to do many of the things you used to do to occupy your time. If medication makes you drowsy or blurs your eyesight, you may not be able to read. Jogging is difficult with a broken leg. But there *are* things you can do. What did you used to do? Which of those are still possible? Think up new activities. Perhaps there are hobbies you always wanted to try but never had time for. Would you like to learn to paint watercolors, refinish furniture, or knit? How about bird-watching, cooking, or writing? Think about volunteer activities you could do.

If you're a friend, ask if the person who's sick needs things to do. Suggest ideas. Perhaps you can bring books from the library; audio or video tapes, including books on tape and relaxation tapes; jigsaw puzzles; board games or cards; knitting, sewing, or art supplies. You might also provide accessories to make those items easier to use, such as a bed table or large board for puzzles, a book-stand to hold books, a bag for knitting. These are small things but it's amazing how often they're neglected. Because it's often difficult to ask for things when you're sick, thoughtfulness and anticipation on the part of friends is greatly appreciated.

Don't forget the professional staff as a resource. Tell your doctor, nurses, and/or social worker that you're lonely or bored; they may have suggestions.

ANGER

You didn't choose to be sick — and anger is a perfectly normal reaction. In addition, being sick is sometimes painful, scary. lonely, and downright inconvenient. All the more reason to be angry.

"One of the things you feel with cancer right from the beginning is a fantastic amount of anger that this has happened to you."

"You get angry over the lack of insight that other people have about you, especially people who know damn well you're sick."

"I was so miserable that nobody wanted me there. I wasn't pleasant to anybody. I was yelling at the nurses, I was mean to the doctors."

"I was angry with Chuck for not being there. I felt it was his duty to come and be with me but he didn't even call. I was downright angry."

CAUSES AND TARGETS OF ANGER

Anger can be at the nurse who physically hurt you while giving you an injection or who doesn't poke his or her head in the door the moment you ring the buzzer; at the doctor who's never around when you want him or her, or who doesn't explain enough, or who doesn't have a cure; at the friend who doesn't visit, doesn't visit enough, visits at the wrong time, or says the wrong things when he or she does visit; at the motorist who hit you; at all auto companies; at God; at yourself; at almost anyone and anything.

You may be angry at a friend's or spouse's response to your illness.

"Gary thought that being sick was a real cop-out. He used to get angry at me, even though I was ill and there were very real

things wrong with me. I had pneumonia for two weeks and lost 25 pounds and had a fever of 104°. I just got chastised and bitched out. Nobody called the doctor, nobody helped me. He thought I was just being a hypochondriac. I almost died."

"Here I was, really sick, and my wife didn't come to visit me much. She said she had to care for the kids. I was furious; I needed her."

Life doesn't stop for everyone else when there's a sick person in the family. Life, ordinary life, goes on. Family members still go to work or school; holidays and birthdays still occur; movies and favorite TV shows still exist; and the dog still needs to be walked. This can create conflicts — and resentment.

"There was real resentment about my having left her to go visit my grandparents ... and real resentment for my insisting on singing in the opera." [from a man whose wife had a broken leg]

Medical people are often the targets of anger. Sometimes they're just an easy, available target. Sometimes it's because they don't live up to our unrealistically high expectations of what they can do. We may be disappointed to discover that doctors are no more perfect than the rest of us and that they too sometimes make mistakes, get tired, or simply don't know everything. Sometimes doctors really do mess up — and there's no excuse for their poor performance or their mistakes. Unfortunately, with illness the stakes can be high: mistakes can mean discomfort, pain, and even death.

"This burn on my arm was caused because the doctors didn't want to take the trouble to find a room where I would lay down and take the chemotherapy by slow intravenous drip — they wanted to shove in into my arm fast. So now I have a chemical burn and a messed up wrist. All of that is sheer stupidity, but they were making decisions based on their convenience or ignorance. The result was substantial damage to me."

"After the cataract operation the surgeon told me there was a dull blade. I just blew up. 'You convinced me to use this hospital because it had the most complete and extensive equipment and you tell me the reason I nearly lost my sight is because of a dull blade!'"

Such stories are endless, even if not every one we hear is accurate. Sometimes the anger is totally justified and sometimes not. Where is the line between human fallibility, the limits of a complex medical care system, a science that still has many unknowns — and malpractice? This is an issue that will be argued in the courts for a long time — and the answers aren't always clear. But our first reaction is often anger, regardless of whether the problem is malpractice, lack of caring, an honest mistake due to the imperfections of medical science, lack of a good bedside manner, brusqueness due to overwork, the innate imperfections of human beings, or just not being omnipotent and able to fix everything and meet all of our needs.

Perhaps the most difficult anger for anyone (family, friends, or medical staff) to receive is undeserved anger. While I was working at the hospital, one bedridden man threw his full bedpan at a nurse for no apparent reason. Another woman began screaming at her nurse as the nurse walked into the room.

Although some people seem to have the patience of a saint and others, such as nurses, are trained to help them understand and tolerate such actions, no one ever likes to be the object of undeserved anger, even if they understand what caused it. And so the people who receive this anger, who are abused in this way, sometimes react by being nasty themselves — or by staying away.

A third party can sometimes be helpful in these situations. Janice, the woman who screamed at her nurse, was sorry immediately and admitted to me that she wasn't angry at the nurse but was simply so alone and frustrated that she just exploded. She also realized that yelling at the nurse just pushed her away more, which was exactly the opposite of what Janice, who desperately needed friends, wanted. She decided to make a big effort to change her actions and try to control her frustration and unhappiness and to reach out to people. I persuaded the nurse to give her another chance and it worked. The man who threw the bedpan was not so fortunate. He wasn't able to change his behavior (the bedpan incident was the worst of a long series of incidents) and the result was that he was a very unpopular patient and was ignored by the staff as much as possible.

Sometimes anger is easier to express than other feelings — and it can mask other feelings. Anger at the guy in the next bed who has noisy visitors all day may in fact be envy that he *has* visitors while you don't. Anger at a nurse's brusqueness may reflect loneliness and a desperate need for more human contact. Anger may mask fear or frustration. Or it may be easier to yell at a nurse than to admit your dependency and ask for something. Anger may also mask hurt. One woman described her response to the fear of being abandoned by her boyfriend.

"How dare you do this to me, how dare you leave me, how dare you abandon me. So I'll be mad at you first. And I'll show you, I'll leave first."

Sometimes even when there is a real cause for anger, the torrent of harsh words that pours out is an accumulation of frustration and other built-up anger. Perhaps a nurse takes a little too long one night to bring pain medication and the patient, who has been waiting anxiously, explodes — angry at that particular nurse but also angry at all the other nurses, doctors, and orderlies, or even at a spouse or friend. So that unfortunate nurse may receive far more than his or her fair share of blame.

Anger is sometimes misdirected because some people feel safer getting mad at someone they know well. Others feel safer getting mad at a hired nurse. Perhaps they trust those people to be more understanding (or hope they will be) or they have less fear that those people will get mad and desert them if they get angry. Perhaps in the case above the nurse who was slow to bring medication was actually one of the better nurses, one who did seem to care about patients, who did see them as people, did care about their needs, and who was almost always available when needed. Perhaps the patient got mad at this nurse precisely because she knew that nurse would understand her anger better than some of the other nurses. But if you're that nurse, that's still hurtful, even if you understand it, especially when you're proud of the work you do and want to be appreciated for it.

Family and friends sometimes get an extra load of anger directed at them for this same reason.

"None of her anger and none of her unhappiness ever came out towards people she didn't know real well, it only comes out directly at people she does know well. Times when she said she was frustrated at her physician, instead of dealing with the doctor, she'd take it out on me."

And, of course, friends are bound to do something wrong at some time — because of ignorance, because their needs conflict with yours, or simply because they're not perfect.

Sometimes it isn't possible to confront the real culprits. Perhaps they're inaccessible or finding them would take a lot of investigation. The nurse who was slow to bring your pain medication may have been swamped with several crises at once, perhaps in a hospital that was understaffed because of budget cuts made by a distant bureaucracy. Some problems are simply unavoidable. A well-staffed and well-run ward can be hit by an unusual number of crises one night — something that's just not always possible to predict and prepare for.

Anger can be a frightening emotion for the person who's angry, as well as for the object of the anger. We're sometimes afraid to let out the anger we feel inside. Perhaps it might explode, get out of control. Sometimes we're even afraid to acknowledge there's any anger inside at all: we hide it from ourselves.

"It's very hard for me to accept that my anger isn't something I can rationally control. But because I think I shouldn't be angry doesn't do any damn good."

And if we get angry how will the people we get angry at react? Will they yell back? Will they go away? We don't really want to lose them, especially when we're sick and may be dependent and needing friends.

> *"I was so angry but when I'd verbalize my anger that would make him angry and he'd stay away even more."*

So even when the anger is justified, it may be difficult to get angry at the doctors, nurses, family, or friends who have so much power over you. The patient who explodes, or who even gets very calmly and rationally angry risks being avoided by the medical staff, or by friends and family. So there's a real incentive to try to hide the anger, even if it doesn't work in the long run.

HOW TO DEAL WITH ANGER

What can you do with your anger? Holding it in generally doesn't work for long — and it probably won't even make you feel good in the short run.

> *"We're both afraid to get angry at each other, yet I know if we keep it hidden it will just keep growing like a balloon and finally explode."*

You can try to be clear about your anger, express it as best and as constructively as you can, and explore its underlying causes.

HOW TO DEAL WITH ANGER

1. Clarify your anger — and the facts.
2. Express your anger:
      — if justified, express it clearly
      — if unjustified, vent it harmlessly.
3. Explore and deal with the underlying causes.

---

1. CLARIFY YOUR ANGER

Who or what are you are you really angry at? Once you figure that out, ask yourself if they were aware of what they were doing?

Did they do it on purpose? This is also the time for a reality check. Did they *really* do what you *think* they did? If not, it's always good to clear up misunderstandings.

Take another look at the facts. Is the situation really as you see it? Are you making unfounded assumptions? Can you look at the situation from the other person's point of view? Can you talk with them to clarify the facts? Friends can sometimes help you get a clearer perspective.

2. EXPRESS YOUR ANGER

If the anger is justified, it may help to get it out directly to the appropriate person as calmly, clearly, and constructively as possible. If the night nurse gave you a shot that hurt, talk to him or her about it and see if there might be a solution for the future. Then maybe you won't get angry at the day nurse on the next shift.

Expressing your anger is taking action. You're doing something, and that in turn can decrease some of the frustration and powerlessness that might have contributed to the anger .

Even if your anger is unjustified, it sometimes helps to express it out loud to anyone willing to listen, or say it to a tape recorder, or write it down. Physical exercise or even hitting a pillow can help let off steam. Getting the anger out is usually better than keeping it bottled up inside. Even if you can't express your anger to the right person, at least try to be clear at whom or at what you are angry. Perhaps the process of getting out the anger will allow you to discover if there are other emotions hidden underneath.

3. EXPLORE UNDERLYING CAUSES

If the anger is unjustified, it may actually come out of other emotions — primarily frustration and powerlessness, but also dependency or fear. Understanding that and then dealing with those other emotions might decrease the tendency for it to come out as anger. Look closely at your anger. Is it masking other feelings, such as hurt, fear, or disappointment, that you might be able to deal with more directly?

Even when the anger is justified, the intensity of it may be due to other reasons.

FOR FRIENDS AND FAMILY

For those who aren't sick — family, friends, and medical staff — it may help to remember that anger directed at you might really be intended for someone else. Anger and verbal abuse is never pleasant, and simply understanding won't solve that (nor do I want to condone it). But understanding the anger may allow you to be a little more patient, and not take it personally. Perhaps you can help the person who is sick to deal with their anger instead of only reacting to it. Just listening and caring may help.

GUILT

If you can't get angry at other people for your illness, maybe you should be angry with yourself. Maybe it's *your* fault.

Guilt is a complex feeling that can be set off by many things — past or present, real or imagined. Guilt implies that you should be doing something differently or should have done something differently in the past. There is a delicate balance between feeling guilty and taking responsibility for your actions.

KINDS OF GUILT

It's easy to feel guilt about your illness — either 1) guilt for causing the illness, 2) guilt about healing, and 3) miscellaneous guilt.

1. GUILT FOR CAUSING THE ILLNESS

You may feel guilty for things that happened in the past. "Did I cause the illness or injury in some way?" "Perhaps I shouldn't have been driving when I was so tired." "If I had settled down and gotten married like my parents urged, it wouldn't have happened." "Perhaps I haven't been eating well enough." "I should have quit smoking." "I've been eating too many potato chips and candy bars." "I didn't go to the doctor soon enough." "Maybe my job is too stressful." "Perhaps if I'd gone to church every week...."

It's endless. If only you — or they, or someone — had done something different, it wouldn't have happened, or at least it might not have happened, or wouldn't still be happening. Hindsight always seems so clear. Sometimes what we did or didn't do really might have made a difference — but we sometimes feel just as guilty if it wouldn't. Guilt is no more rational than other emotions.

CAUSATION

Before focusing on the guilt surrounding an illness, let's look at the actual causes of illness. This is a tricky question and scientists are constantly refining — and changing — their theories. There are direct and indirect causes; obvious and subtle ones; primary and secondary causes; and clear, indisputable ones and unproven but possible ones. So the question of how responsible we are for our illness (or healing) gets very complicated.

Finding the causes of illness (and accidents) will keep scientists (and lawyers) busy for years to come. Preventing diseases assumes that medical science clearly understands their causes. But scientists will tell you that, although there are things they do know for sure, there is much more that is only vaguely understood at this time, much that is disputed, and some that is still a total mystery.

Ironically, some relatively recent discoveries can create guilt. Due largely to a great deal of cancer and AIDS research, scientists are learning much more about the workings of the immune system. One result is that psycho-neuro-immunology (PNI) is now recognized as a special field with its own name and a growing body of research and literature. Although this is tremendously useful in treating and preventing illness, it also has great potential for causing guilt. If there is a mind/body connection, did I make myself sick? Should I be able to make myself well?

Information on the role of nutrition and environmental poisons (including such commonly used substances as alcohol, tobacco and pesticides) in contributing to or helping prevent certain diseases can also increase our guilt. While current research on genetics and heredity is bringing exciting new discoveries, these also have potential for creating guilt, even though we can only act on the basis of the best information we have at any given time. Discovering that your illness is hereditary or contagious can lead to guilt that you may have passed it on to others, unintentionally or before you knew you were ill.

Rather than seeing these possible causes of illness as reasons for guilt, it may be more useful to rejoice: as scientists solve more puzzles, we'll learn more ways to improve our health.

2. GUILT ABOUT HEALING

Once you're sick, another area of guilt comes into play — one that focuses on the present and not the past. "Am I doing everything I can to get better fast?" "Am I following the doctor's orders to the letter?" "Am I eating the right foods." "Have I gotten the best possible medical advice?" "Is there anything else I could be doing?" Trying to figure out exactly what you should be doing is hard because science isn't perfect and experts' recommendations sometimes change or even conflict. What if you're trying to do the right thing but can't figure out what it is?

This power to affect your illness can create conflicts with friends and relatives — and medical staff. Friends and family usually want you to get better and they may make you feel guilty, unintentionally or on purpose, if you don't do what they think you should.

> *"My wife and my therapist implied it was my responsibility to make myself better by changing my personality, by radical breaks with the way I had been before, by adopting new lifestyles. It became more and more of an assault on my identity."* [from a man with advanced cancer]

Family and friends obviously don't want you to suffer, or to die (in cases where the illness may be that serious). They don't want to lose you. They fear loss, and they may get angry — and scared — if you do anything they perceive as harmful. You and they may have differing ideas about how much control you really do have over your illness. Food, rest, and exercise are fairly easy to monitor and measure but psychological attitude and the "will to live'" or to get better is much harder to measure and control.

Not being able to conform to all the restrictions placed on you by an illness, and therefore feeling you are setting back the healing process, can lead to guilt. Someone on a very limited diet may eat forbidden food on occasion, sometimes paying an immediate price (if the food upsets a delicate digestive system, for example) or an unknown future price (if you eat too much fat or if you smoke). Someone with an injured leg may walk on it a little too much, perhaps causing more hurt or delaying healing.

We all have expectations about how we should cope with illness — expectations from our family and friends, doctors, society in general, and from ourselves. We feel we should live up to those expectations. So, in addition to dealing with the illness, we're often constantly aware of how we *think* we should respond to it. If we don't measure up, we may feel guilty.

3. OTHER GUILT

There are also other causes of guilt. There can be guilt for causing so much trouble. If you inconvenience others with your illness, you may feel apologetic. And there's guilt for causing pain and worry for others.

"I worried a lot about the amount of pain I was giving to people close to me. You start apologizing for being sick."

"I found out that my mother had been waking up in the middle of the night, crying a lot, because of me. I wish I could spare her."

Because of your illness, your family may have to change their lives, sometimes fairly radically. There may be guilt for the time, money, and attention that you're diverting from other people and other needs.

If you've survived an accident or an epidemic (such as AIDS, for example) that killed others, you may suffer "survivor guilt." Why should you be healthy, or alive, when others weren't so lucky?

You might feel guilty about some of the feelings you are having. If you feel relief or joy, you might feel guilty for not suffering enough (or not suffering as others may expect you to). Or you might feel guilty if you get angry at those who are trying so hard to help you.

HOW TO DEAL WITH GUILT

The first step in dealing with guilt is to learn to recognize it — both inside you and also when others lay guilt on you. Let friends and family know when they do things — either inadvertently or on purpose — that make you feel guilty.

In general, guilt is only useful when it motivates action — when it helps you learn from your mistakes, spurs you to reach your goals, and keeps you from doing things you shouldn't do. But you also have to recognize that you're human and that no matter how hard you try, you won't be perfect. Don't berate yourself for that. Avoid setting impossibly high standards that you can't live up to and accept that you're bound to make some mistakes. Focus on the positive things you can do.

HOW TO DEAL WITH GUILT

First, learn to recognize it. Then:

FOR PAST GUILT:

The past is past — let it go. But use it:
— to learn from
— to motivate changes.

FOR PRESENT AND FUTURE GUILT:

Guilt is useful only to motivate you to do better.
1. Set realistic expectations.
2. Make the best decisions you can.
3. Take good care of yourself.
4. Help others avoid your mistakes.

Since there are different types of guilt — about the past or present — let's look at them separately.

GUILT ABOUT THE PAST

Guilt about the past is useless — unless you can learn from it or if it motivates you to change your actions in the present and future. Use the positive, constructive guidelines that can come from discovering the causes of your illness — but don't get bogged down in the unconstructive morass of feeling guilty for past mistakes or for things beyond your control. In other words, learn any lessons you can, but then let it go. We all make mistakes, although some are more costly than others and some are more avoidable and downright stupid. But they are all still past. Blaming yourself will only take energy away from more important things.

Since it's easy with hindsight to criticize past decisions, it might be useful to ask yourself whether you would make the same decisions if you had it to do over again. If so, does that make it any easier to accept the past? If you would do things differently, can you make those changes now? Can you help others learn from your mistakes?

GUILT ABOUT THE PRESENT AND FUTURE

Guilt about the present is also worthless, unless it can motivate you to do better. Set realistic expectations, make the best decisions you can, take good care of yourself, and help others avoid your mistakes.

1. SET REALISTIC EXPECTATIONS

Guilt arises when reality doesn't live up to expectations — and you take responsibility, or blame yourself, for the shortfall. This disparity can be caused by expectations that were too high as well as by your failure. If you can't be as cheerful or self-sufficient as you'd like when fighting a serious illness, the problem may be your expectations, not your performance.

Expectations are often useful: they reflect goals, values, and standards and they can provide something to strive for, even if you don't always succeed. To decrease guilt when reality doesn't meet your expectations, you can change either the reality (your actions or feelings) *or* the expectations.

The next question is whose expectations are you trying to meet — yours or those of other people? Your expectations should reflect *your* goals and values. Separating what you really feel and what you expect of yourself from the expectations of others can be a step to reducing guilt caused by others. If you think you should be doing things differently, you might want to try to change. But if you are satisfied with what you are doing — have faith in yourself. It's your opinion that matters most. Don't try to live up to the expectations of others if you don't agree with them.

To set your expectations:

A) Be clear about your values, goals, and standards.

B) Set expectations for yourself that are based on *your* values and standards (not someone else's).

C) Set realistic expectations.

D) Do your best to meet those expectations — but remember that while expectations are goals to strive for, you're only human and won't always meet them 100%. Don't expect perfection.

E) If you fall short, re-evaluate your standards, set more realistic short-term expectations, or try harder in the future.

2. MAKE THE BEST DECISIONS YOU CAN

Examining your decisions (and making them consciously and carefully) and examining the values on which they're based is the first step towards reducing guilt in the present. Guilt isn't rational (or logical) so you may still feel guilty — but examining all this may at least make you realize how irrational the guilt is and help you make better decisions.

Since you can't make good decisions without good information, obtain the best information and help you can. Then make your decisions based on that.

Life is filled with choices. We constantly make decisions and take risks, large and small, and do things we may pay for later. Every time we cross the street we take a risk that we may be run over by a car. But most of us cross streets (and some who stay inside are killed in their homes anyway). All decisions involve some risk, so evaluate the risks and make the best decisions you can — but then make your peace with your decisions, accept the consequences, and go on with life.

3. TAKE GOOD CARE OF YOURSELF

Take care of your body and follow your doctor's treatment orders as best you can.

There are a lot of specific ways to improve your health and decrease chances of illness or accident. You can avoid harmful foods and drugs as much as possible. Since it's now clear that smoking causes cancer, heart disease, emphysema, and more, you can stop smoking. It may not be easy — but it can be your goal. You can change your diet, get enough exercise, and decrease the level of stress in your life. You can avoid as many pollutants as you reasonably can. As scientists discover more about how your body works and what causes illness, you can take advantage of new medications and treatments.

But no matter how hard you try, you won't be able to eat the perfect diet, get the exact amount of exercise and rest, avoid all bad stress (but allow the right amount of "good" stress). In part you won't be able to do that because no one knows for sure just what the "right" way is. And it may always be like that — so relax, do the best you can, and go easy on yourself.

HELP OTHERS AVOID YOUR MISTAKES

Although it may be too late for you to change a decision, perhaps others can benefit from your mistakes. What can you do to aid that?

Illness and accidents are caused by so many things that to tackle the causes may seem overwhelming. But things do change — and even one person can make a difference. One woman whose daughter was killed by a drunk driver began MADD (Mothers Against Drunk-Driving), which now has many chapters nationwide. MADD is having a huge impact on anti-drunk-driving legislation and enforcement with the result that we now have many fewer deaths and injuries due to drunk-drivers. One man who learned about the dangers of saturated oils after he had a heart attack began a very successful publicity campaign that has resulted in some major companies removing saturated oils from cereals, cookies, movie popcorn, and fast foods.

There are endless stories about the difference that one person can make. And you don't have to act alone — there are many groups you can join to work with others to improve the world. Even small individual actions, such as never driving while intoxicated, being kind to others, and even just smiling, can help too.

One person who goes into a classroom and talks about AIDS or who teaches their own children about health and how to care for their bodies is helping. One person who gives money to help medical research is helping. One person who volunteers with an organization such as the Cancer Society or their local hospice or hospital is helping. One person who pollutes the earth less (by recycling, not smoking, or conserving energy and other resources) is helping.

There are many ways to help. You can take individual actions and collective ones, large and small. You can work within your schools, workplaces, organizations, and government for changes that affect health, such as tougher drunk-driving laws, smoking restrictions, and pollution controls; better health education and health insurance. You can also work for better preventive medical care and better pre-natal and infant care for everyone, regardless of income.

If guilt motivates you to do any of these things, you'll help make the world a better place. And you can do them even if you don't feel guilty.

THE GOOD NEWS: BENEFITS OF ILLNESS

"After a while I got very high while I was in the hospital. I could feel that I was going to change my whole life. I didn't know how or what, but it was very clear to me that I had to do something. It was very powerful and exciting. When I was lying in bed in that hospital, somehow I was able to see things a whole lot clearer about myself. There wasn't the usual static going on — kids and the house. And there wasn't a lot going on in my head. I could really focus on what it was all about. I remember thinking that I was seeing things very clearly."

Although illness is generally a difficult time, good can also come from it. Although few of those I interviewed for this book voluntarily mentioned any positive effects of illness, I found that when I specifically asked about benefits, most found some — although there were a few emphatic "no's." Sometimes the answer would be a grudging "I guess so," followed by details of some new things learned. Sometimes a person would discover a positive aspect to something that had previously been seen as completely negative. Other times the answer was a resounding "yes" and the person talked excitedly of the good things.

Some people expressed a great deal of joy at some of the new discoveries they had made because of the illness. These benefits included: 1) a change in their values or in the direction of their lives, 2) an increased understanding of themselves and other people, 3) a new appreciation of life and the good things they did have, 4) an awareness of how much they were loved by their family and friends, 5) an awareness of their inner strengths and resources, and 6) motivation and information to live a more healthy life. And finally, interspersed with all the difficult emotions, there were also some positive ones — joy, love, pride, excitement, and sometimes relief.

1. CHANGES IN VALUES AND LIFE GOALS

Sometimes illness, especially serious illness, forces us to look at our lives and reassess our goals and our values. Most often the people I interviewed talked about this aspect of illness as a wonderful experience — one they were very thankful for. I sometimes think that illness can be our body's way of telling us that we need to make a change in our lives. Illness often forces us to make changes we had perhaps failed to make earlier. In this sense, illness can be a "blessing in disguise."

"I was working in the family business and I never really faced the fact that I wasn't too happy. I worked like hell. What the heart attack did was it said to me, 'You're not immortal, you're not going to live forever, and if you want to make some of those changes rattling around in your head, you'd better start.' Sometime after that I quit the job. I became more conscious of relationships — my kids, my wife. It refocussed me. If I hadn't had the heart attack, I would have just gone right on."

"I realized that I had to re-assess my whole life, the meaning of my life. I had not been a good student. I was putting all my energy into physical things and I'd fallen way behind. I was in the lower half of my class going into the senior year. After the crisis, I began taking studying more seriously."

Work and career goals are often the first thing that are examined as part of this re-evaluation, but friendships, family, and marriage are also often considered as well. And as people changed their values and goals, the quality of their lives often also changed.

2. GREATER UNDERSTANDING OF YOURSELF AND OTHERS

Illness can bring you an increased understanding of yourself — and others. Sometimes this is due to the inescapable emotions that surface with illness, the shock of facing your mortality, the strength gained from meeting the challenges of illness, and sometimes just from having time out from the normal rat race which can allow time for introspection.

This increased awareness may also lead to greater compassion for others. Some people talked about gaining a new perspective on life, becoming less self-centered and more aware of other people and their problems.

"I guess I'm selfish. The first couple weeks I thought only of me. Then, when I could get around a little, I realized that there were people a lot worse off than me. And they were somehow coping. I'm lucky, I just have a broken leg and it will heal."

"It made me more aware of other people's problems. When you're sick, your life becomes centered around certain things, like a wheelchair. After being in that wheelchair for a week, I notice wheelchair access wherever I go."

3. APPRECIATION OF LIFE

Adversity often makes us appreciate the good things we do have, and illness is no exception. We appreciate simple things we took for granted and never noticed.

"I used to complain so much, I never thought I'd miss going to work — but I do. I miss the chaos and the craziness."

After a few days in the hospital, the sky seems bluer, the sunsets redder, and the birds sing more sweetly. Corny, but often true.

4. LOVE AND FRIENDSHIP: STRENGTHENED RELATIONSHIPS

"It was painful but there was so much closeness it was incredible.... We cried a lot but we laughed a lot too." [from a man whose wife was dying of breast cancer]

"I understood in ways I had never understood before how much Arturo loved me and how important I was and that what happened to me really mattered to him."

"It made me closer to some people. Friends came to the hospital all the time so there were some people I saw much more than I would normally see them. It deepened some friendships, affirmed others."

"My family has gotten much closer to me. I needed them and they came through."

"I made some wonderful new friends in the hospital who I still see."

Illness often makes people more aware of their relationship to others. For some this meant becoming more aware of their aloneness and lack of close friends and family — but others realized how many good friends they did have and how many people really cared and came to their aid when they were in need. Some made new friends or deepened existing friendships and drew closer to loved ones. Sometimes it's the intensity of emotion that exists with illness, the lowering of defenses, or the fear of loss that makes you realize just how important someone is to you. Sharing emotions and feelings, with or without illness being present, almost always strengthens bonds — and simply lets you get to know someone better.

You may develop a new appreciation of the institutions of marriage and family (or friendships) and the support they provide. You may also become more aware — and appreciative — of the people involved — people you may have underestimated or taken for granted before the illness.

"One pleasure among the pain has been ...feeling that there's no one imaginable we'd rather go through this with than each other." [from a couple dealing with their child's cancer]

"It's been great in some ways. It makes me slow down and be with my daughter and play with her quite a bit more than I had been. We've been spending a lot of time together. She's been able to do a lot of things for me."

"Somehow we managed to stick it out together and in the process grew together." [from a man with severe diabetes about the early years of his marriage]

"It brought out the good things. Ever since we haven't been living at home, my sister and I haven't had much time together. But being sick, with my parents away at first, it was just Janet and me and it was real good. It was wonderful. She got to feel like this big sister, which she hadn't been for a long time. I got to feel all this respect for her."

5. INNER STRENGTH

"If I can live through this, I can live through anything."

Just as illness can make you aware of your vulnerability, it can also make you aware of your strength, and even bring out that strength. When faced with a difficult situation, we often rise to the occasion — and are surprised to discover the inner resources we have. The increased confidence and self-esteem from that discovery can last a lifetime and can help you cope with many other adversities.

We often underestimate our own ability to cope with illness (and perhaps with any hardship). As difficult as it may seem beforehand, when you're actually confronted with such a situation you generally discover resources and strengths you never knew you had. When I first began interviewing people for this book, I frequently thought, "I could never do that; I could never deal with those illnesses," and I was often in great awe of those people. But when I stopped to think about it, almost everyone who was sick would have said the same thing — before bad luck or circumstances forced them to deal with their accident or illness. I would never have predicted that I'd deal as relatively easily with cancer as I have.

A woman suffering from an undiagnosed but very debilitating illness told me that if she was still in the same condition in six months, she'd kill herself. She then paused and went on to add:

"If someone told me six months ago that six months from then I'd still be dealing with this, I'd never have believed it. Human beings are strong — I keep pushing back my suicide date." [Postscript: I found her 18 years later, still coping. She had totally forgotten about the suicidal thoughts of the past.]

6. HEALTHIER LIVING

Illness often gives you both additional information to improve your health — and motivation. Learning about your body can lead to long term improvements in your health and/or the health of your family.

"I take care of myself in ways I didn't used to. I eat better, I get exercise, I try to do things that make me feel like my life is worthwhile. That's been the biggest change in my life."

Although information about health and particular health risks is now much more available — it's hard to watch the evening news or pick up a magazine without some medical news — illness may give you information that's very specific to your particular situation. At a time when we are bombarded by so much information on health that it's hard to know what's most important, illness can help you pinpoint the priorities for your body.

Many of us know we should be eating better, but old habits are hard to change. Illness may motivate you to make some changes you've long known you should make. A brush with illness may make you realize that the pleasures of smoking (or the difficulty of breaking the addiction) or your high-fat diet just aren't worth the dangers. After an illness, it's harder to feel invulnerable and justify bad habits by saying, "It won't happen to me."

POSITIVE EMOTIONS

Although negative feelings may predominate, and will usually get more attention, illness can also bring out positive emotions; and these are perhaps even sweeter because of their rarity. Many people I interviewed expressed joy at the changes and discoveries mentioned earlier. Illness can also produce excitement, awe, pride, and relief.

EXCITEMENT AND AWE

Laughter peps you up — but so do feelings of excitement and awe that can come from learning new things — about health and illness or about yourself — and from the challenge of combatting an illness. Let yourself be excited and challenged.

Illness can be a "learning experience." You'll learn how to enhance your and your family's health. Some people are even motivated to change their career and learn new skills as a result of their illness. This book began as a result of things I learned during my father's open-heart surgery years ago. I became intrigued and pursued the subject. When I got breast cancer, I discovered the immune system, which I had known almost nothing about before. I became fascinated by the sophisticated inner body network that keeps us healthy — and proceeded to create first a film and then a book about it (*The Immune System: Your Magic Doctor*). I feel much richer because of the many things I learned from illnesses — and much better able to stay healthy in the future.

PRIDE

The realization that you're coping with a difficult illness can make you feel proud of yourself, perhaps proud of newly discovered strength or skills. You may also be proud of the way your family members have responded.

RELIEF

"Initially for me it was kind of a break. You're suddenly relieved of all responsibility, I had a room of my own. People showered me with books and things."

Illness is stressful — but it may also bring relief from the stresses of your normal life. It may be relief from an unpleasant job, from a painful family situation, from general worries, or simply from coping with the complexities of life. Or illness may simply be a welcome break, even if life isn't all that unpleasant. Some people really enjoy the "vacation" aspect of their illness.

"The routine of the hospital is a strange one, but you can get used to it. They come in around 6:00 in the morning, Some people find it offensive; I loved it. I loved getting up that early. In fact, I'd try to get up earlier. I'd be up about 5:30 and ring for the nurse. She'd bring me a cup of hot coffee and a towel. I'd wash myself off, have my cup of coffee, and I'd read and turn my radio on low. It would be dawn, the sun would be coming up and it would be lovely. And it's so quiet in the hospital at that time of day."

"You get into this habit of doing whatever you please and not being answerable to anyone."

"I became a spoiled brat. I was totally dependent and I abused it. I asked for everything; I didn't know when to stop."

"There are some seductive things about being sick, that are superficially positive but can be dangerous. Like giving yourself permission to take it easy in ways that can become habitual. You drift into doing much less than you could do. You develop a stake in your invalid status."

You may get more attention when you're sick, feel more loved and cared for, get less pressure and more leisure time. That can be very seductive — and can even be an incentive to be sick. Perhaps if we could find ways to get more of that in our daily lives there would be fewer sick people in the world.

Sometimes the illness itself may bring relief from uncertainty. For one man, an appendectomy meant the end to the uncertain state he lived in before the operation, even though he had complications from the surgery and a difficult recovery period.

"When I was having chronic appendicitis, I didn't go anywhere. Always in the back of my mind was, 'Is there a hospital around so in case this thing pops I can have it cut out?' After it was out, I could eat anything, go anywhere. I really felt freed up."

When a mammogram discovered the tiny cancer in my second breast and I decided to have a second mastectomy, I did so more with relief than anything else. The cancer wasn't a metastasis (spreading) of the first but a totally new one so I didn't worry about further spread of the cancer. I took the new cancer as proof of what I'd suspected and feared all along — that I had a high risk of developing cancer in my remaining breast for the same reasons I got the original cancer. Since I'd always known I could develop cancer in the second breast I'd been watching very carefully to be able to catch a tumor early if it did develop. Now it had happened and I actually felt safer and more relaxed after the surgery.

A diagnosis can bring good news. Before the diagnosis, your imagination can run wild and you fear the worst. It can be a relief to find out that things aren't as bad as you feared — that you don't have some dreaded fatal disease, or the broken bones are healing better than expected, or an operation won't be necessary after all. The illness or limitations you do have may then be more easily tolerated.

Finally, obtaining a diagnosis after a long period of simply not feeling well but not knowing why, can also be a relief and may finally give you a clear direction in which to proceed, even if it's not a pleasant one. Once you know what is wrong, there will be specific things you can do. And that gives you more power.

HOW TO MAXIMIZE THE BENEFITS

Although illness brings both good and bad, the bottom line may boil down to whether you generally look for the good things in life, or whether you always focus on the dark side. People are different by nature. Some will find the good in almost any experience, while others never seem to see it even when it's right in front of them. But we can all change. We can look for the positive side — and even create it.

HOW TO MAXIMIZE THE BENEFITS

1. Look for the good that exists. Make lists.
   — What have you gained and learned?
   — How has life changed for the better?
2. Create positive benefits. Go over the possibilities in this chapter and see if you can make some happen.
3. Appreciate the benefits.
4. Now go back over your list and see how you can get those benefits *without* being sick.

---

1. LOOK FOR THE GOOD

Look for the good — it will help balance out the bad. I realize that's not always easy — and you may have to look hard. When I would ask about good things during my interviews, many people were surprised I would even ask such a question. Others had to think a few moments. But once asked, most did find benefits. And they were glad I asked because it made them realize there *were* good things. So ask yourself, or your sick friend, about the good things. List the benefits that have come from your illness— what you gained and learned and how your life has changed for the better. Perhaps you won't find anything to put on your list — but you may also be surprised at what you *will* find.

2. CREATE POSITIVE BENEFITS

Create good things. Take another look at the different sections of this chapter and if they don't yet apply to you, see if you can make them happen. Work to strengthen friendships or create new ones, work to increase your power and strength, learn more about how to keep your body and mind healthy.

3. APPRECIATE THE GOOD THINGS

Appreciate and enjoy the good. Do more than grudgingly acknowledge the existence of the positive benefits you listed above — or the good things in life in general: take a little time to think about them and appreciate them.

4. GET THE BENEFITS WITHOUT BEING SICK

Then go back over your lists and think about how to obtain all those benefits without being sick!

Section III

SPECIAL PROBLEMS: PRACTICAL SOLUTIONS

CHANGES IN DAILY LIFE

Illness, by its very nature, affects the essentials of life — walking, moving, talking, eating, breathing. Some parts of your body probably won't function in the same way as before, either temporarily or permanently. But life is a lot more than just walking, eating, and breathing. It's what you do with your time — work, friends, and your other interests and pleasures. When you're sick, all those things are affected as well. In this chapter I'll look at how illness affects: 1) economic survival (including work, money, and living situations), 2) the use of your time and energy, and 3) relationships.

If reading about all these possible effects of illness is too depressing right now, you may want to read this chapter piecemeal — perhaps first skipping the problem descriptions and going straight to the suggestions for how to deal with them. Later, reading about the problems may give you validation and additional insights.

1. ECONOMIC SURVIVAL

WORK

"For 6-7 months I went to work every day but terribly sick, barely making it through the day. Finally in April I couldn't do it any more and went on medical leave. My leave is up in November and I'll lose my job if I'm not back — and I have no way of knowing whether I'll be well enough."

Work is an important part of our lives. We've already seen how it can be a source of self-worth, purpose, and identity. It can also be a source of challenge, stimulation, and fulfillment, as well as simply a source of income. Even if work is dull, it keeps us busy, structures our life, and provides opportunities to meet and interact with people.

A serious illness may force you to change your job, or perhaps to stop working completely, either for a period of time or perhaps forever. That's enough to be a major blow even to someone in excellent health. Retirement can also have a disastrous effects on people who have geared their entire life to working, but with retirement you have the advantage of being able to plan ahead. Illness doesn't give you time to plan; all of a sudden it may force you into retirement, or perhaps a period of unemployment or curtailed activity.

Even if your illness doesn't require you to cease working completely, it can affect the type of work you can do.

"I couldn't do any physical labor. I could no longer depend on my body as a means of making a living. I was furious." [from a truck driver with a bad back]

"I had both feet operated on when I was in nurses training when I was 17 and it completely turned my life upside down. There weren't so many jobs for young women in those days. I was told I could finish training but could never do floor duty in a hospital, so it played havoc with my career. It was a long time before I was able to work at all." [from a woman with rickets]

"A full day's work is out of the question, in terms of my energy level and the amount of pain I have and the amount of painkillers I have to take, which slow you up." [from a man with cancer]

As disruptive as it is, having to change your line of work can have a bright side. It can lead you to discover new jobs and new careers — or new hobbies and interests. It may be an excuse to try something you've always wanted to do.

HOW TO DEAL WITH WORK PROBLEMS

Solutions to many of the daily life problems are very practical ones. Once you determine how much and for how long your illness will affect your ability to work, you can begin to plan alternatives. You may be looking at short-term adaptations or long-term career changes. Explore your options. Talk to people, brainstorm, and make lists of what you can and can't do — and also what you'd ideally like to do.

HOW TO DEAL WITH WORK PROBLEMS

1. Make a list of what you can and can't do
   — and what you'd really like to do.
2. Brainstorm and explore all resources.
3. Explore adapting your current work.
4. Explore new careers.

---

1. MAKE A LIST OF WHAT YOU CAN AND CAN'T DO

Make a list of the things you can no longer do because of your illness — and of what you can do. Then begin another list of things you'd really like to do. If you haven't thought about that in a long time, your list may start out small. But keep it handy and keep adding to it as you think of more things. Your first task is to compile as long a list as possible. Later you can narrow it down.

2. BRAINSTORM AND EXPLORE RESOURCES

Brainstorming with family and friends can be key. Based on their knowledge of you and their different perspective on the world, they may suggest things that you would never have thought of.

Explore all resources that might help you. Social work services may be helpful — they've had experience solving similar problems. They may know about disability benefits, retraining and job counselling programs. They can also often help you plow through medical, insurance, and government bureaucracies.

3. CAN YOU ADAPT YOUR CURRENT WORK?

Consider ways you can adapt your current work, as well as totally different options. Do you want to continue your present job or line of work? What would you need to be able to continue?

4. EXPLORE NEW CAREERS

If you can't continue your old line of work, you may need to explore what work you could do. Go back and expand the list of what you'd like to do Be idealistic to begin with; then you can be practical and see how the list translates into jobs. Talk to job counsellors if possible, including about any retraining programs for which you might be eligible.

MONEY PROBLEMS

It's a peculiar contradiction. If I stay alive for a long time, I'm going to be in an economic crisis, unless I get so much better that I can go back to work full-time. But the stress of my job hurts the cancer. It's a bind; you're trapped.

When a job is your source of income, obviously losing it means less money (or no money at all) for your family. Other members of the family (if there *are* others able to work) may have to look for work or increase their workloads. Sacrifices may have to be made. Less money may mean a less expensive apartment or house, in a less expensive neighborhood, and/or a different style of social life. It may even mean applying for government assistance, which is both meager and demeaning.

"It sapped our finances. We eventually had to sell our house."

"Mark wanted to go to college but now I've used up the money we had set aside for him. He's had to get a job because I can't."

The effect on your current finances can range from the minor inconvenience of using up money you'd been saving for a vacation or a new car to requiring major changes in lifestyle due to decreased income. Medical costs can also affect your future by wiping out retirement savings or creating debts that will take years to pay off. Or they can affect the lives of others by taking money earmarked for a child's college education or money from family or friends.

"I just can't afford to be sick. I can barely pay the bills as it is."

Even if you don't lose your job, illness costs money and can drain financial resources. We hear horror stories about high medical costs, but we assume that always happens to others — we never expect it to happen to us. While many people have medical insurance, growing numbers don't have any. And some who have insurance lose it when they become sick because the company cancels the policy or they can no longer afford the premiums. Government safety nets are grossly inadequate, leaving many people with no protection at all.

Even for those who do have insurance, there may be very large deductibles and loopholes. Some insurance policies, for example, don't cover medications, nursing homes, home health care, physical therapy, psychologists, nutritionists, special diets, non-traditional medicine (such as acupuncture or herbal medicines), new or experimental treatments, or sometimes even doctor visits and tests— all of which can be expensive. Some insurance limits which doctors, hospitals, or treatment programs you can use. Most policies have a lot of fine print, including deductibles, upper limits of coverage, and co-payments. If you haven't carefully reviewed your insurance policy recently, do so now.

Policies that cover only costs if you are hospitalized can be woefully inadequate when so many tests, treatments, and even surgery are now done on an out-patient basis. At the time of my breast cancer, at age 43, I only had hospitalization insurance. Had I preferred to have a lumpectomy (which is followed by weeks of radiation), instead of a mastectomy, my insurance would not have covered the cost of the out-patient radiation, which was then about $8000. I've since changed my policy.

Beyond official medical expenses, there may be costs for child-care, household help, special foods, or transportation. There may also be non-essential but important expenses such as massages, a comfortable lounge chair, or video rentals.

HOW TO DEAL WITH MONEY PROBLEMS

Once you know the extent and medical implications of your illness — how long you'll be sick, how much treatment will cost, and how much your illness will interfere with earning money — you can begin to make serious financial plans.

HOW TO DEAL WITH MONEY PROBLEMS

1. Look carefully at your budget.
2. Identify places to cut expenses.
3. Check your insurance carefully.
4. Explore all resources that might help you.
5. Brainstorm to increase your income.

---

1. LOOK CAREFULLY AT YOUR BUDGET.

If you don't have a clear idea of where your money goes, write it down. Add in every expense, even the little things. Include all the changes due to you illness — either decreased income or increased expenses. If you think about the possibility of illness before you get sick, you can plan for it by keeping some money in reserve and procuring good insurance coverage.

2. CUT EXPENSES.

Once you have an accurate budget, you can begin to identify possible places to cut. Be creative. Are there possible ways to increase your income? Are you looking at permanent adjustments or short-term increases.

3. CHECK YOUR INSURANCE POLICY.

Check it very carefully. Find out exactly what is and what isn't covered. Talk with people experienced in dealing with insurance, such as hospital social workers or your doctor's staff. They sometimes know how to define what you need so it falls within the limits of insurance policies. If you're not sick — check your policy now and make sure you're adequately covered.

4. EXPLORE ALL RESOURCES.

Explore any applicable government or private programs. Here again, hospital social workers can be useful. Can family or friends help financially if necessary? This may be a difficult area to discuss, especially when pride is involved — but remember that being sick is not your fault.

5. BRAINSTORM.

Think of any creative ways to increase your income. Ask friends to contribute their ideas.

LIVING SITUATION

Long illness or disability may mean a change of residence, for financial or health reasons, or to be closer to caregivers. You may need to move to a warmer or dryer climate, someplace with cleaner air, or a different type of house or apartment (smaller or larger, with better heat, a spare room for caregivers, wheelchair access, or no stairs). You and your family may suddenly be uprooted from home, friends, a neighborhood, and perhaps a job and other family members. For some people moving is exciting and fun, an excuse for change, and a challenge. For others it's lonely, painful, and stressful.

You may need to move, temporarily or permanently, because you need more care than you can obtain at home. You may need to move in with a relative or to a nursing home or convalescent hospital. As difficult as those moves may be, obtaining the care you need may be well worth the move. Hospitalization entails a change of residence, at least temporarily, with new, rigid routines and a lack of privacy.

Sometimes a move can be carefully planned but it may also come abruptly, with the person concerned having very little control over what's happening. One big city hospital nurse told me:

"They came into the hospital and the next thing they knew their stuff was being put into storage, they had lost their home, lost their jobs, and had not the slightest idea of what was going to happen to them when they got out of the hospital. Those are the people who fall through the cracks."

Yes, there are people who fall through the cracks, who don't have anyone to take care of things for them if they become seriously ill. It's a sobering thought, and one to think about — and, if possible, do something about — before you get sick.

Although there are many important problems that may need to be solved, such as who will care for the children and the house while a single parent is in the hospital, sometimes it's the little things that matter.

"I've got my clothes and furniture in a friend's garage — but there was no one to take my kitty. I had her for six years. I miss her so." [from an older woman who lived alone before she was hospitalized]

HOW TO DEAL WITH YOUR LIVING SITUATION

When you have to consider changing your living situation, think out exactly what you need and evaluate your present situation and possible alternatives carefully. There may be various ways to meet your needs.

HOW TO DEAL WITH YOUR LIVING SITUATION

1. Look carefully at your present situation.

2. Brainstorm and evaluate possible solutions.

3. Prioritize your needs and desires.

4. Explore all resources that might help you.

---

1. LOOK AT YOUR PRESENT SITUATION

If your present living situation doesn't work as it is, perhaps there are ways to make it work rather than move elsewhere. Can you re-arrange rooms or furniture? Sometimes moving a little furniture around can make life much more pleasant. Can you turn a first-floor dining room into a bedroom until you can climb stairs again? If you live alone but need extra care, can a friend move in for a while?

2. BRAINSTORM.

Brainstorm and evaluate possible solutions. Be creative.

3. PRIORITIZE.

Prioritize your needs and desires. Be clear about what things are most important to you.

4. EXPLORE RESOURCES.

Explore all the resources that might help you. Consult with social workers or others who have experience resolving such problems — they may have creative suggestions and they may also know of resources to help meet your needs.

2. TIME AND ENERGY DRAINS

TIME DRAIN

> *"Then there's entering into the world of being a patient. It's like a part-time job. I easily spend 20 hours a week between seeing three different doctors, the cancer psychotherapy program, and physical therapy for the destruction that the chemicals have produced in my body — plus the times I was so terribly sick from the chemotherapy."*

Being sick takes time — so much sometimes that being sick can seem like a job in itself and may greatly interfere with your "real" job or other activities.

When I discovered my first breast cancer, I had two weeks between the diagnosis and surgery. I was trying to meet a writing deadline and hoped to use that time to finish a lot of work before the surgery since I wasn't sure how usable my arm would be immediately afterwards due to the removal of armpit lymph nodes. Instead, I ended up spending most of my time talking to doctors to decide on the best course of treatment, getting lab tests to determine if the cancer had spread (it hadn't), reading about breast cancer, and talking to many friends. In addition, and at the urging of my doctor, I made extra time for exercise and relaxation, which I had been neglecting because I had so much else to do.

Diagnosing and treating your illness (doctors' visits, lab tests, and/or various treatments) can account for a lot of that time. Learning about the disease, in order to make informed decisions and to be sure you're getting the best possible treatment, also takes time. And simply talking to friends — about your feelings, the latest medical details, or their concerns — is also time consuming. All that leaves you exhausted and with less time for other things.

Having a large circle of friends and family can be wonderful, but it can also be time-consuming. Friends of mine whose child had cancer wrote a letter to their friends, in part to deal with this problem:

"One unexpected stress of the whole affair, indeed, has been responding to our friends — for this distress is not Laura's and ours only but vibrates through so wide a web that we would have caved completely from the dear and dreadful task of telling hundreds one by one the basic tale, let alone daily updates."

ENERGY DRAIN

I made a point to go downstairs every day to get my mail. Just that tired me out. [from a man with a broken leg]

Illness not only takes time, it also takes energy — both physical energy and emotional energy.

PHYSICAL ENERGY

The healing process is fascinating. If you're aware of the many complex processes going on inside your body, you'll more easily understand why you feel so tired.

When you're sick, the immune system works overtime to destroy unwanted invaders (such as bacteria, viruses, or cancer cells) — and many new cells must be created to replace damaged ones. This uses up much of the energy that you would normally use for other things. The result is that you feel tired and need extra rest and nourishment. The tiredness you feel forces you to rest so your body can have more energy for healing.

Respect your body's need for rest and nourishment. The more you learn about how the immune system works, the better you'll be able to help it.

EMOTIONAL ENERGY

"The other very difficult thing about being sick is that you're obsessed with it. It makes discussions about other things hard to deal with."

Illness consumes so much energy that it can easily become the focal point of your life. It can occupy most of your time and become the major topic of conversation, sometimes to the exclusion of other subjects or activities. Even the attention you receive when you're sick consumes energy.

"As kind and wonderful as visitors are, they're real energy drains. It takes a lot of energy to be nice and smiling."

"I got mail, flowers, and phone calls to the extent that we finally had to turn off the telephone. Everyone was wonderful, but I just couldn't do it."

A plea to friends and family: don't let these comments keep you from visiting or calling, but do be sensitive to the needs of the sick person.

HOW TO DEAL WITH TIME AND ENERGY DRAINS

You may not be able to do everything you used to do in addition to all the new things the illness requires. That's OK. Respect your limits. And get help.

HOW TO DEAL WITH TIME AND ENERGY DRAINS

1. Know your limits.
2. Budget your time and energy.
3. Prioritize.
4. Get a little help from your friends.

---

1. KNOW YOUR LIMITS

Superman and Wonder Woman are cartoon characters; real people can't do all those things. Be aware of your limits — especially when illness is draining your resources.

2. BUDGET YOUR TIME AND ENERGY

Budget your time and energy. Think out what needs to be done on any given day. Make lists. Then figure out how much energy you realistically have — and what kind of energy. If there's more to be done than you can possibly do, read the next steps.

3. PRIORITIZE

Prioritize what needs to be done. Everything isn't equally important. Don't just plunge into tasks — figure out what really needs to be done, and what can only be done by you. Be sure to include some time for pleasure and rest.

4. GET A LITTLE HELP FROM YOUR FRIENDS

Ask your friends for help. Remind friends of what you do and don't need. If you have a community of friends and family, mobilizing them all will spread out the burden — and it may also let each of them feel that there is something they can do to help. One person can take the initiative and organize the others. Make a list of what needs to be done, and ask others to volunteer for specific tasks they can do.

Friends and family can help conserve precious energy by collecting information, doing errands and household chores, fielding phone calls from others, and giving updates. If there's a large circle of friends, a formal phone tree or a letter to friends (giving medical information and also saying what the sick person needs) might be appropriate.

EFFECTS ON RELATIONSHIPS

The pressures and intensity of illness will almost inevitably affect your relationships with family and friends in some way. Since I've already looked at the beneficial effects that illness can have on relationships in Chapter 12, I'll concentrate here on the stresses.

STRAIN ON FAMILY

"As the illness progressed, I was no longer able to take care of myself and it placed more and more responsibilities on her shoulders." [from a man dying of cancer]

Illness will affect relationships with a spouse or with your family as it puts new pressures on the relationships. Sometimes the pressures are external, caused by financial hardships or life-style changes. But often the pressures are internal, caused by the problems and emotions generated by an illness — the dependency, the feelings of fear, worthlessness, anger, and depression.

Sometimes simply maintaining a relationship or maintaining the same level of closeness is difficult when families are separated by hospitalization.

"We went from being together all the time to a half-hour visit a day, assuming I could get there every day."

Just the constant presence of illness strains a relationship.

"You're obsessed with being sick. It makes discussions about other things difficult."

Sometimes families can meet the increased needs — and sometimes they can't. The discovery that one partner may be unable or unwilling to provide what the other needs or wants can cause disappointment and anger. What the sick person needs is also not always what friends and family give. Sometimes it's that we often give to others what *we* would like to receive — which may not be what *they* want. If we'd like to be left alone, for example, that's how we respond when someone else is sick, even though they may prefer companionship and backrubs.

Illness can accentuate or draw attention to existing problems in a relationship and the additional stress caused by the illness is sometimes more than an already strained or weak relationship can stand.

Sometimes illness forces us to re-examine the level of commitment and caring we have for each other. "In sickness and in health" is often simply an empty phrase to those who are young and healthy. We often don't understand what it can mean until we actually face the reality and the stress of sickness.

Problems may surface that had been invisible before. Illness may force a couple to examine what it was that brought them together in the first place and what continues to hold them together. A man who was attractive because of his status and ability as a good provider may become less attractive if he looses those qualities — and he may be very aware, and afraid, of that. A woman who was attractive because of her strength may appear very differently when she feels helpless and has needs that she wants and expects her partner to fulfill.

"He had never liked to deal with me when I was sick and it always put a tremendous strain on our relationship. What he had always seemed to love in me was my strength and independence and aliveness. He didn't want a dependent person and I became an incredibly dependent person when I was really sick. I wasn't the person he wanted me to be. It's easy to see now why the relationship was having trouble."

Her husband knew his wife's illness had severely damaged their relationship.

"She was deeply angry and very bitter. It's been a recurring theme in our relationship that, 'You've never been there.' Both times she was sick she didn't feel she got the support from me that she needed."

In addition, you may no longer be able to do many of the things you enjoyed together. People may realize that marriages, or friendships, were based on flimsy grounds, perhaps too flimsy to continue. They may find that there wasn't enough to hold them together through hard times, that their spouse or friend didn't or couldn't meet their needs, and that they were perhaps even better off alone.

Sometimes illness forces us to deal with aspects of one another — both good and bad — that we've been able to ignore during normal times. The demands of an illness might lead to new respect, appreciation, and closeness — or it could destroy the delicate balance in a relationship that had barely held together before that.

Even if illness causes a relationship to collapse, that may have a positive side. Although the timing may be unfortunate, the collapse of a weak and unsatisfactory relationship can sometimes provide an opportunity to begin anew — either on your own, with another person, or even with the same person, basing the new relationship on the reality of who you both are at the present time. Although with hindsight some people talk about these types of life changes as generally positive in spite of the hurt, this is not likely to be apparent when you're caught up in it. During an illness, the breakup of a relationship is just an added burden at an already difficult time — and another loss at a time when you already may have many losses.

Since doctors often see only the medical side of an illness, if you have complex family problems, make sure the doctors (or social worker, if available) and family and friends understand these and take them into account.

SEX

Most illnesses affect sex — either sexual functioning itself, sexual desire, your general energy level, or the opportunity for sex. Hospitalization only compounds the problem, regardless of how you feel physically, since a hospital is obviously not the ideal place for sex, or even for more modest intimacy. Even with a private room, there's a definite lack of privacy, since medical staff don't always observe "do not disturb" signs. And then there's the narrow beds and lack of romantic atmosphere. This may seem trivial but it can become very important if you spend much time in a hospital.

Even outside the hospital, sex suffers.

"I can't move — how can I think about sex?"

"I'm on so many drugs that I'm constantly drowsy, sometimes nauseous. I can't imagine making love."

In another case, the tender areas were totally unrelated to sex, but even so:

"The most blatant effect is on our making love. I was so afraid of causing pain by touching her the wrong way. I had to be very self-conscious of how I touched her and that was a real strain."

If the illness itself doesn't affect sex, sometimes the medication needed to treat it will. And stress, preoccupation with illness, and low energy levels are not at all conducive to sex or romance.

FRIENDSHIP

Although illness will naturally affect close family relationships the most, it will also affect friendships. Although illness can affect friendships in a positive way (see Chapter 12), it can also harm them .

"You sure find out who your real friends are."

"I've lost a lot of friends who were very important to me."

Friends whom you hoped and expected would be helpful and supportive may not be for a variety of reasons. They may have other commitments that prevent them from being with you. Or they may be uncomfortable around illness, or frightened by it. Perhaps it reminds them of their own vulnerability or mortality. Some people stay away because they don't know how to cope with dependency, anger or any of the other emotions of illness. Perhaps they're overwhelmed by *their* emotions.

"You experience other people's fear of you. A number of close friends have not called me or made any effort to get in touch with me for months and I know the reason is fear. They can't cope with their fears of cancer and they're terrified. They don't know how to relate to me so they don't."

"A lot of friends were very scared that I was dying or something, They didn't want to get near it."

Perhaps friends fear that a visit will be depressing or that they won't know what to say or how to act. They may not know what you want and need. Some people especially dislike hospitals or "sick rooms." I used to have so much trouble being around people in pain that I'd actually get nauseous visiting anyone in a hospital. This feeling went away only when I forced myself to overcome it while doing research for this book, and even then I sometimes had to leave a hospital room to go out for a short walk or breath of fresh air before I could continue.

Some "fair weather friends" are lost forever; others return later in the course of the illness or when the illness goes away.

Some friendships wither because you're no longer able to participate in your old activities or your old job. In our work-oriented society, friends are often formed at the workplace and sometimes that's the main source of contact with those people. So the loss of a job may mean the loss of friends and companionship.

"The loss of work friendships was a terrible loss, but there wasn't enough of an outside relationship developed to sustain them. A few people still call me."

"I'm less in contact with the people who gave me feedback, my co-workers. People I used to see 3-4 times a week I don't see more than twice a month — and that makes a big difference."

And sometimes, consciously or not, you'll push people away.

"The stress was really showing in my relations with friends. I was bitchy and crabby and feeling under tremendous duress."

Someone who's sick often simply isn't great fun to be around and friends may have to be patient and understanding. Many will, but some won't.

HOW TO IMPROVE RELATIONSHIPS

Above all, remember that this is a difficult time. Stress will disrupt things — and that's normal. But this is also an area where there are many ways to improve relationships, especially with talking, openness, patience, and understanding — and sometimes with a little professional help. And make an effort to spend some pleasant time together.

HOW TO IMPROVE RELATIONSHIPS

1. Talk openly and directly about the pressures and needs you all feel.
2. Be gentle and understanding.
3. Get help if you need it.
4. Spend pleasant time together.

1. TALK

Talk with your friends and family. Talk about your (and their) needs, fears, hopes, and pressures.

Talking necessitates good communication. This assumes that people know how to communicate in a clear, straightforward way, which, of course, is not always the case. We're not born knowing how to communicate well — it's a learned skill. Don't expect others to be mind-readers.

When communication is bad, one person can greatly improve the process — whether that person is the one who's sick or a friend or relative. If you're sick you can have a lot of control over communications because you have the power to set the tone, to ask for or demonstrate what you need. You can set a tone of openness and directness that will influence those who look to you for clues on how they should act. You can let people know it's OK to talk about both the technical details of your illness and the emotions you're feeling. You can also let them know if there are things you don't want to talk about at any particular time. You can try to be open and direct. You can let people know your feelings and your needs. You can interject humor — or seriousness.

2. BE GENTLE AND UNDERSTANDING

Keep in mind that this illness is difficult for your family and friends as well as for you. Let them have time for themselves and don't expect them to do everything. There may just be too much to do.

3. GET HELP IF YOU NEED IT

If the illness is causing serious problems in your relationship with family or friends or if you have trouble communicating with anyone (family or doctors), ask someone else to help — including professionals such as social workers, family therapists, clergy, or your doctor. It may be helpful to find someone who's familiar with the problems and pressures created by illness.

4. SPEND PLEASANT TIME TOGETHER

Look for things you can do with friends that are mutually satisfying. If the things that you used to do together are disrupted by the illness, find new ones — whether it's talking, watching a movie, playing chess, or walking in the woods.

FOR FAMILY AND FRIENDS

As a friend, you can let the sick person (or other family members) know that you're willing to listen and talk. If you spot any of the problems mentioned in this section, maybe you can step in to clarify things and improve the communication. Sometimes an outside person can spot a communication problem that the people involved don't see. Maintaining good, clear communication will be a big help in any illness.

PAIN AND DRUGS

It's not possible to talk about illness without talking about pain and drugs. Illness doesn't have to involve pain, or significant pain, but for those who do have it, the pain can be a central, or perhaps *the* central, part of the experience.

PAIN

Pain adds a whole new dimension to illness. The pain can be excruciating or just uncomfortable; it may be predictable or irregular; it may be constant or intermittent; it may be long-term ("chronic") or short-term ("acute"); it may be controllable by medication or other means, or it may not. If drugs are used to control the pain, then the drugs and their side-effects can become yet another problem to deal with (see p. 193).

Severe pain hurts: but more than that, it can become the focus of your waking hours — and it may mean you have few sleeping hours. Pain — even simple discomfort — draws attention to your body, sometimes making concentration on other things difficult. And focusing on it may lead to even more awareness of it and "feeling" more pain. It can become a vicious cycle.

Pain can block out other feelings and thoughts. It can make you not want to talk or be with people or do much of anything. Pain distorts your world.

"It's so easy to lose perspective when you're in a lot of pain."

"That kind of pain is so totally exhausting, so energy-draining."

Severe pain often brings with it the specter of death.

"I guess I didn't believe that something could hurt that much and not kill me."

Even when the degree of pain is not severe, it's mere presence is disruptive. It's a reminder that something is not right with your body, even if what's wrong isn't at all life-threatening.

"Think about having a toothache, and think about having it constantly for a year. It's not going to kill you but you can't live properly with it."

"For people who have chronic pain, it's like a prism of a particular kind through which you are viewing the world. It makes you feel very different and strange."

"The pain isn't severe; I just can't ever get comfortable — not in any position, not in months." [from a man with colon cancer]

Even if you have no ongoing pain, you may constantly be aware that if you twist your arm, leg, or back the wrong way, you may bring back an old pain — so you're always cautious, and you're constantly thinking about it.

When I had tennis elbow, my arm didn't actually hurt most of the time, as long as I avoided using it. And even when I accidentally used it the wrong way, the pain wasn't that great. But I was always afraid I might be surprised by a sharp pain. And, probably more important, I worried that the pain was a sign that I was doing more damage to my arm, which meant it might take longer to heal or might never heal properly. So for a long time I was very protective of my arm, afraid of touching a sore spot or re-injuring it.

PERCEPTION OF PAIN

We don't all perceive pain in the same way. Different people may report the same level of pain very differently — or the same person may perceive the same pain differently at different times. This may be due to your expectations, your physical tolerance level, and how much control you have over the pain.

We all have different levels of tolerance to pain and different expectations. Some people think suffering is a part of life that should be ignored if possible or otherwise borne stoically; others expect to always be totally pain-free and are surprised and upset by minor aches.

A key factor that seems to affect our perception of pain is whether we have any control over it. Inability to control pain seems to make it worse. But often you *can* do things to alleviate the hurt, with either non-medical remedies, medication, or other medical means.

PAIN AS A WARNING — OR A NATURAL PROCESS

Pain can be a signal from our body that something is not right. A stimulus, such as pressure or heat, causes a nerve to send a message to our brain, which the brain interprets as pain. So pain can actually be seen as a warning to let us know that we should do something to correct the problem, such as pull a finger off a hot stove, remove a swollen appendix, or reset a broken bone.

Pain can also be a part of a natural process. Pain in childbirth comes from muscles and skin stretching to allow the baby to be born. If you hit your thumb with a hammer, the injury and natural healing process will cause the thumb to swell, the skin will be taut, and it will throb. Most of these natural processes will go away on their own and do not need to cause anxiety.

We might fear pain less if we all had a better understanding of what it is; how it works as a warning; how it is a part of some natural processes, including healing; and the wide variety of ways we can reduce and control it.

KINDS OF PAIN

Doctors divide pain into two main types:

1. Acute pain — short-term pain that will either get better naturally or can usually be successfully treated with either medication or surgery.

2. Chronic pain — long-term pain which is often more difficult to treat. It may be reduced or come and go, but it never goes away completely.

CONTROL OF PAIN

No one likes pain — and when you have it you want to be able to decrease or end it. Most pain, especially acute pain, can be controlled. Pain is managed differently depending on whether you're in the hospital or not, and whether the pain is acute or chronic.

Pain management today is much improved over the past — both the techniques of pain control and the philosophy that underlies it. Most doctors no longer believe that patients should be stoic about pain, that certain effective medications shouldn't be used because of the possibility of addiction, or that infants don't need pain control because they don't feel pain. All that is (or should be) past and you should complain loudly if your doctor hesitates to give you effective pain control without a good explanation. You have the right to be as pain-free as possible — and to be involved in the decisions about how to balance the advantages and disadvantages of various forms of pain control.

Although when most people think of pain relief, they think only of narcotic or non-narcotic medications, there are many varied ways to control pain — including: 1) pain relief medications, 2) other types of drugs that can have some pain-relieving effects, 3) other medical methods of pain control, and 4) non-medical methods.

When dealing with pain, you should look at *all* possible options — in fact, successful control of pain will often involve a combination of several methods.

PAIN MEDICATIONS

Different drugs work in different ways. The main types of pain medications are:

1. **Non-narcotics.** Often called NSAIDs (nonsteroidal anti-inflammatory drugs), these common analgesics work at the site of the pain and relieve pain and swelling. They include aspirin and ibuprofen (Motrin, Advil). Their main disadvantage is that they interfere with blood clotting and may cause nausea, stomach bleeding, or kidney problems. Also included in this general category is acetaminophen (Tylenol), which works differently and thus avoids most of the above side-effects, but must be used with caution by people with liver problems.

2. **Narcotics.** These opioids (including morphine and codeine) are effective for severe pain and are frequently used short term, for example after surgery. They affect the central nervous system and our perception of pain. Although they can create dependency and are potentially addictive, they seldom create problems with short-term use. (For more on drug side-effects and addiction see p. 193.) These often have a sedating effect that you may either appreciate (if you have a lot of pain or trouble sleeping) or resent (if you want to be alert, read, or work).

Pain and pain control is often a cyclical routine. Pain medication is often given as needed, with limits set on frequency. As the medication wears off, the pain begins anew. Then more medication is given. It would be simple if you could always take a pain pill that would end the pain immediately whenever any pain became too severe. But for many reasons — including side-effects, the possibility of addiction, and simply the logistical problem of taking the medication so that it kicks in at just the right time — that isn't always possible. So pain control is balancing act.

Because doctors now recognize that it's best to keep pain levels low, they often prescribe medications on a regular schedule rather than having you wait for the pain to return before asking for more relief. This schedule should be adjusted to meet your needs. Another alternative appropriate for some drugs is a PCA (patient controlled analgesia) pump that feeds the medicine through an IV line and that allows you, within limits, to regulate your own medication.

OTHER MEDICATIONS SOMETIMES USED FOR PAIN

There are also other medications that are not exclusively pain-killers but may be useful for specific types of pain:

1. **Steroids** (including Cortisone and Prednisone). These are anti-inflammatory drugs that are seldom given for acute pain but may be used for chronic pain. They can have serious side-effects and must be used with caution and careful supervision.

2. **Antidepressants.** Depression doesn't cause pain (although long-term pain can cause depression) but it can accentuate your perception of pain and make it harder for you to deal with the pain. For that reason, treating depression can be helpful for pain. In addition, some antidepressants have a sedating effect that may help when pain disrupts sleep. Anti-anxiety medications (Xanax, Valium) can sometimes also help, especially for acute pain.

3. **Muscle relaxants** — useful for pain associated with muscles but they affect the central nervous system and can have unwanted side-effects.

4. **Anticonvulsants** — useful when there is injury to a nerve.

5. **Antacids** — useful for gastric pain.

6. **Local anesthetics** (such as novocaine used by dentists and epidural blocks for childbirth). These block the nerves that transmit pain signals and are given by injection near the site. They are used primarily for short-term pain relief during surgery.

NON-DRUG MEDICAL METHODS OF PAIN CONTROL

Other medical, but non-pharmacological, approaches to pain relief include:

1. **Acupuncture.** Thin acupuncture needles, inserted (and sometimes heated or twirled) at specific "acupuncture points," have been used in China for centuries to alleviate certain kinds of pain and are now used more in the U.S..

2. **TENS** (Transcutaneous Electrical Nerve Stimulation). These are small, portable battery operated units that deliver a low electrical charge through a couple strategically placed electrodes attached to your skin surface. They may be useful for certain kinds of pain.

3. **Cutting nerves.** Cutting a nerve that transmits pain signals to the brain will stop you from feeling that pain. This can be effective for some localized pain that doesn't respond to other treatment.

OTHER TECHNIQUES FOR PAIN CONTROL

Sometimes non-medical solutions are very useful, including many techniques you can do yourself or with the aid of a friend.

1. **Ice or heat.** Ice reduces swelling and also numbs the affected area. Heat relaxes muscles and can loosen stiff arthritic joints. An easy way to use ice is to freeze water in a paper or styrofoam cup, then hold the cup and peel it back as needed to expose the ice. Menthol creams (Ben-Gay, Mentholatum, Tiger Balm) can create a soothing sensation when applied to the skin.

2. **Relaxation.** This can mean relaxing muscles and also your mind. It can include breathing exercises, meditation, bio-feedback, Yoga, relaxation audio tapes, self-hypnosis, and visualization. These can be extremely valuable and generally easy to do. There are many books and classes that teach various techniques.

3. **Massage.** Gentle massage can be soothing and deeper massage can relax muscles.

4 **Distraction.** While this won't actually reduce the pain, it can help you notice it less. This can include music (including headphones during a procedure), conversation with friends, work, television, or a good book. Laughter can be especially helpful.

5. **Exercise.** Exercise releases chemicals in your body, called endorphins, that are natural painkillers. Proper exercise can also help restore weak or damaged muscles.

Ask you doctor if any non-drug solutions could be useful for your situation. If your doctor doesn't know, do some research. And try asking a nurse.

WHAT YOU CAN DO ABOUT PAIN

If you have pain, work with your doctor to clarify the source of the pain and explore all possible options for pain control. Don't tolerate more pain than necessary but if you must live with chronic pain, don't let it take over your life.

WHAT YOU CAN DO ABOUT PAIN

1. Discuss the pain with your doctor.

2. Clarify the source of pain.

3. Explore options for pain control.

4. For acute pain — Try to obtain the
    best pain relief you can
    — and don't be a martyr.

5. For chronic pain — Don't let the
    pain take over your life.

1. DISCUSS THE PAIN WITH YOUR DOCTOR

Pain and pain management are important parts of illness and you should discuss them with your doctor and nurses. Nurses can be especially important because they deal with pain every day and can often make helpful practical suggestions.

As you discuss your illness or a specific procedure, ask what you can expect in terms of pain — although remember that not everyone will experience pain the same way. Let your doctor know how much pain you're feeling, what level of pain you are willing to tolerate, and how you'd like to deal with pain. Some people don't mind a little pain and prefer it to the side-effects of medication. Ask ahead of time if a procedure may hurt and what to expect, so you can prepare yourself and try to remain relaxed.

If you have pain, you might want to keep a log book, describing the pain as clearly as possible (pressure, throbbing, sharp, dull...), when it occurs, what drugs you're taking and any side-effects, and how the pain responds to medication or other treatment. This can be especially useful, both in diagnosis and in fine-tuning medication, since the doctor isn't around all the time and your log book might be more accurate than your memory.

2. CLARIFY THE SOURCE OF PAIN

Knowing the source of your pain, if that is possible, is the first step in deciding how to treat it. Is the pain due to intestinal gas, swelling of a particular area, or tense muscles? If so, this may point to simple ways to relieve the pain. Is the pain accentuated by anxiety that you might be able to reduce?

3. EXPLORE OPTIONS FOR PAIN CONTROL

Discuss the different options available to control your pain with your doctor. If you need pain control, is there something that will affect the source of the pain? Aspirin or ice, for example, can reduce inflammation while an antacid can reduce gastric acidity. Other medications, such as morphine, blunt the perception of pain very effectively but don't address the cause of the pain, although they may be very effective for post-operative or other acute pain that will diminish naturally. Since certain drugs are especially useful for particular types of pain, your doctor may use a combination of drugs to control various aspects of your pain.

If you're taking pain medication that makes you feel drowsy, try adjusting the dosage or the type of medication (in consultation with your doctor). You want to find the best balance between being knocked out by pain and being knocked out by the drugs. It may be difficult, but search for the best balance you can find. Remember that the more control you have over your pain medication, the less you may need to take (and thus the fewer side-effects you'll have).

Check out non-medical methods of pain control. Some are very likely to be helpful, either instead of drugs or in combination with them. These are generally easy to do and low-cost, and with few, if any, risks or side-effects.

There are times when it's difficult to obtain complete pain relief, either with medication or other remedies. Sometimes we don't have effective medication or can't use it for a variety of reasons, such as allergies, fear of addiction (for certain people), or harmful or very unpleasant side-effects. And some pain is just very difficult to control. In those situations, although some pain may remain, you may be able to make it more bearable by distraction, relaxation, or other means. Explore any techniques that may help. For stubborn chronic pain, you might want to check out the options provided by a pain clinic that specializes in the management of chronic pain.

4. FOR ACUTE PAIN — DON'T BE A MARTYR

Try to get the best balance between pain relief and low side-effects. Don't assume you have to be a martyr and live with acute pain — or that there is only one available solution. Modern pain management is much improved — make sure you are aware and take advantage of the new improvements. If you need them, don't avoid narcotics simply out of fear of addiction or dependence.

In spite of all the problems with drugs, using them to block pain can be very useful. When pain is great, it may distract you from dealing with the illness itself. Reducing the pain may then free you to deal with the illness and with the rest of your life. It may allow you to focus on dealing with the sources of the pain or it may let you rest so that your immune system has more energy to fight the illness. And it may simply allow you to enjoy life more.

"When I was in pain and wanted to go somewhere, what I'd do was go anyway and fill myself up with any drug I could fill myself up with that would still keep me conscious and functioning. I was damned if the pain was going to come in the way of my life." [from an older woman with painful arthritis]

Hoping to receive some wonderful philosophical answer, I asked one person, "What got you through the hard times?" The response I got instead was, "Morphine!"

5. FOR CHRONIC PAIN — CONTINUE YOUR LIFE

Although you may find ways to manage chronic pain, it may not disappear completely or forever. Often you will simply have to learn to live with it — and continue your life. Don't let the pain take over. Some chronic pain will not respond to medication, while sometimes the strong drugs needed to alleviate the pain would interfere too much, making drugs not viable as a long-term solution. Management of chronic pain emphasizes the use of non-medical techniques such as relaxation, meditation, distraction, and exercise, along with whatever medications are appropriate. The focus then becomes how to keep the pain from interfering with everything else. If appropriate, check out a specialized pain center. Chronic pain for dying patients is handled differently, with pain relief taking top priority.

DRUGS

Drugs taken to control pain or to cure or manage an illness can add another whole set of problems, especially since they often have unpleasant, or harmful, side-effects. Although illegal drugs can certainly be a problem, I'll focus on the legal prescription or over-the-counter medicines that are most likely to be a problem with illness.

People view drugs differently. For some they're a blessing, for others they're a curse. Most often, perhaps, they're a mixture.

"Those medicines are as energy consuming and attention consuming as the pain itself."

"I hate the drugs. The doctors may not have any choices, but they're really deadly. I don't know what can be done about that. But it sure made the pain stop. It was a miracle. It was the first time in days, maybe a week and a half, that I hadn't been in pain, for 2-3 hours at a time, which seemed like a miracle to me."

"I couldn't sleep on the Talwin. I'd be up all night, but at least I wasn't screaming."

"I guess it's better with the pills than without them, but my mouth is always so dry. It's annoying."

If you're taking medication for your illness, you can assume that some of what you're feeling may be caused by the drug rather than by the illness — but how do you determine what is caused by what? If you're taking several drugs it may be especially difficult to determine which one is causing a particular symptom.

SIDE-EFFECTS OF DRUGS

Drugs often have side effects, ranging from major to barely noticeable. Some medicines are only slightly less toxic than the disease they're treating; some can even be deadly. Some drugs totally disrupt your life or make major changes in it. Some drugs may take away your pain, but leave you feeling out of it, drowsy, exhausted, depressed, or simply not yourself. Even if side-effects aren't harmful or toxic, they may be extremely annoying.

"It totally spaces you out. I couldn't read, I couldn't even watch television. I couldn't focus on anything for any length of time."

You get moon-faced, which is dreadful. You get a round face, your face looks totally bizarre. It's really shocking to wake up in the morning and look in the mirror and all of a sudden your face is really significantly different than the way it normally looks." [from a woman taking high doses of Prednisone]

"I completely lost any sex drive. I was shocked — it never crossed my mind."

CAUTION

Beware of drug interactions. Even though a particular medication is safe, it may react adversely when combined with other drugs, including over-the-counter drugs and legal ones such as alcohol. Ask your doctor or pharmacy about possible interactions and always let them know about all other prescription and non-prescription drugs you're taking. Even drugs that have no known side effects still deserve caution.

Discuss any drug side-effects with your doctor, especially if they may interfere with things you really need to do such as drive, run machinery, read, or think clearly. If you think you may be particularly sensitive — or tolerant — to drugs and therefore may require less or more than normal doses, mention this to your doctor as well.

ADDICTION

Some drugs, including narcotics but also common ones such as nicotine and alcohol, can be addictive. Although attitudes are now changing, for years the medical and political establishments were so overly concerned about addiction that even patients who were dying or in tremendous pain were denied needed medication on the grounds they might become addicted. Since addiction is such a loaded word, it's worth defining it carefully. Drug addiction is often confused with drug dependence and tolerance.

The physical component of what is often loosely referred to as addiction is actually *dependence*. Your body will get used to certain drugs and you'll get withdrawal symptoms if the drug is stopped abruptly. Cigarettes (primarily the nicotine) and narcotics both create physical dependency. Dependence can be handled by slowly decreasing the drug in question when it's time to stop using it. *Tolerance* to a drug means that you need ever higher doses of it to achieve the same effect. Doctors know about these problems and can deal with them.

Addiction is the compulsive use of a drug for its psychological effect. An addict will use a drug even though they have no physical pain and will continue to have a psychological craving for the drug after ceasing to use it. Addiction is a problem when it impairs your health, or your social or work functioning. Addiction, including to illegal drugs, can be a result of a person attempting to cope with and self-medicate psychological pain that could be dealt with more effectively in other ways. Although some people are more susceptible to addiction and dependence than others, the majority of people who need and take medications for pain don't become addicted. Medical attitudes and practice is slowly changing to reflect that. If you're concerned about your susceptibility to addiction, if you have a history of alcohol or drug problems, or if you'll be taking medication for a long time, discuss this with your doctor.

DOSAGES AND BRAND NAMES

Ask your doctor about your medications and dosages. Sometimes the doctor prescribes a certain drug out of habit (or because they've received a lot of publicity or free samples from a drug company). The simple fact that you're interested enough to ask may encourage your doctor to think more carefully about what he or she prescribes. Sometimes the best drug isn't approved by your insurance company (often because of cost). Ask about generic drugs, which will be cheaper but should perhaps be avoided in some specific cases. Your pharmacist can be useful here.

Some drugs, such as Prozac, Ritalin, or estrogen replacements, are controversial — and this information won't be in the printed literature. Ask your doctor if the drug is controversial and what the controversy is.

Drug dosages are not set in stone. Recommended dosages are recommended for the average person — but that dosage may not be the best one for you. Discuss the effects and side-effects of a drug with your doctor so that together you can fine-tune the dosage to suit your body. The doctor can't do this without your feedback.

There may be different ways to take the drugs you need: by mouth (pill or liquid), IV (intravenous, injected into a vein), IM (intramuscular, injected into a muscle), epidural (injected into the spine), transdermal (through the skin, usually a band-aid type patch), rectal (usually a suppository), and nasal (usually a spray). If you have a choice, discuss the pros and cons with your doctor.

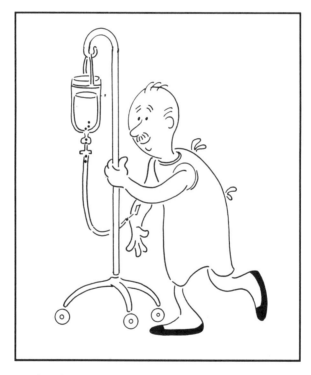

Always take drugs as prescribed — and for the length of time prescribed (unless you check with your doctor). Stopping some medications abruptly or prematurely can be harmful. If antibiotics, for example, aren't taken for the prescribed period, some bacteria may remain (although your symptoms may have disappeared) and come back stronger and more resistant to medication later.

EXPERIMENTAL DRUGS

Sometime the best drug for your illness isn't available, or at least not in the United States. Because of the long and complex Food and Drug Administration (FDA) testing process, new drugs take a long time to be approved. Some drugs aren't produced commercially because the testing and production process would be too expensive ("orphan drugs," for example, for diseases affecting relatively few people) or because of political reasons (for example, the "miscarriage" pill RU 486).

Some new drugs and treatments are available through special research programs before they are available commercially. Ask your doctor if there are any programs that would be appropriate for you.

Some helpful drugs are illegal despite the fact that some people have legitimate medical need for them. Marijuana, for example, has been proven useful to minimize the effects of nausea associated with cancer chemotherapy and to increase appetite (with AIDS and cancer, for example) — but it's still illegal.

WHAT YOU CAN DO ABOUT DRUGS

To make your experience with medications as good as possible, learn about the drugs you're taking and work with your doctor.

WHAT YOU CAN DO ABOUT DRUGS

1. Become informed about drugs, including dosages, side-effects, and interactions.
2. Keep a record of your medications with you.
3. Work with your doctor as a partner.

   — Discuss drugs with your doctor.

   — Keep track of effects and side-effects.

   — Help your doctor fine-tune dosages.

---

1. BE AN INFORMED CONSUMER

Learn as much as possible about the medicines you take, dosages, their effects and side-effects, and interactions with other drugs. Doctors and nurses are obvious sources for this information. Pharmacists are also very useful since they are drug experts — and, although they don't know your particular case history, they are often more accessible and have more time than doctors if you have questions. If cost is an issue, tell your doctor.

The *Physicians' Desk Reference (PDR* for short) is a valuable book used by doctors and pharmacists. Based on drug company information, it lists every medication, along with complete information about the drug's effects and side effects. Although written in technical terminology for doctors, it's useful and available to the public in libraries and some bookstores. There are also a variety of books written for lay people that present much of this same information in simple terms. Read up on any medication you're taking — and find out about the interactions of various drugs, including over-the-counter and illegal ones.

2. KEEP A RECORD OF YOUR MEDICATIONS

Keep a record of all your medications, dosages, and allergies — and always carry it with you. If you are seeing more than one doctor, make sure they *all* know what drugs you are taking.

3. WORK WITH YOUR DOCTOR

Ask about any drugs you are taking and the reasons for them. Find out how you should take the drug (time of day, with meals or alone) and for how long. Discuss any problems or side-effects of a drug with your doctor — and let him or her know about any other drugs you may be taking as well, including common over-the-counter medications, street drugs, prescriptions from other doctors for other ailments, and alcohol.

Let your doctor know how a drug seems to be working for you. Your input can help your doctor determine the best dosage for your body — to maximize the effect of the drug while at the same time minimizing side-effects. It's a difficult balancing act but one that becomes easier the more you know about drugs and your body. Finding optimum medication dosages will give you more control over your illness — and your life.

DEATH

I've tried to make this book general enough so that people with various illnesses will find it useful. Because of that, I've avoided focusing on any one particular illness, especially illness that leads to death. But some diseases do end in death.

Talking about death may not be easy. Although in recent years it has become more acceptable, for many years death was almost a taboo subject, one that almost everyone — doctors, family, friends, and sick people alike — avoided. Many people are still uncomfortable discussing it.

"I had the same feelings that a lot of his friends had at the beginning — you want to avoid the subject of death. I was really pushing it away in my own mind."

"No one in our family talks about it."

Death is something we all have to deal with sometime in our lives. At some point our family and friends will die — and we'll all die eventually. But dealing with death is seldom easy, especially if it approaches sooner that we'd like.

WILL YOUR ILLNESS END IN DEATH?

While many of us fear death (see Chapter 8), it's important to separate fact from fear. Your doctor is probably your best resource for this, although doctors usually don't like to talk about death any more than the rest of us — and especially don't like to admit that you may not get well in spite of their best efforts.

Doctors are sometimes more comfortable talking openly with families than with their patients so if you have trouble getting clear information from your doctor, perhaps another family member can talk with him or her and then urge the doctor to talk with you directly. Nurses and social workers can also be very useful.

Friends and family can gather information as well as help with communication. Books can be helpful, at least to let you know if death is a possibility with your illness and to perhaps give you some general idea of the probability. But for the books to be useful you need to have a clear diagnosis and a sense of the severity of your disease.

Suppose you've determined that your illness will end in death. How do you know how much time you'll have? Often estimates are simply best guesses, based on averages, and as such are very susceptible to error. While we have statistics about average life expectancy given a certain condition, the course of any given illness in a particular individual is almost never totally predictable. Age and other illnesses must be taken into account. And one hard to quantify factor is the person who is sick and what we commonly call their "will to live" or their willingness to let go. For these reasons doctors understandably often shy away from giving precise information on how long you may live.

Yet for the patient and their family, this may be important information. If it is for you, persevere. No one will be able to give you definite answers but ask your doctors for their best guess. You may not always want to know this information — or may not want to know it now. Family and friends may, however, want the information so they can plan better. In such a case, it's appropriate for them to talk directly with the doctor (although remember that it's usually best to have only one family member act as liaison with the doctor).

You may want information on the expected quality of the time until your death and even on what death itself may be like. Once you have all this information, you can deal with it — in both practical and emotional terms.

HOW TO DEAL WITH DEATH: TAKING CHARGE

"Taking charge" is an optimistic approach, but it can apply to any situation, not just cheerful, easy ones. If you know you have a fatal illness, your goal might be to die the way you want, with dignity — and to live as you want, within the limits of your disease, until you die.

Although we can't ultimately prevent death, we can often have some control over when and how we die. You can have some or a lot of control over the medications you use, where you die (home, hospital, hospice), who will be with you, and sometimes when you die. And you can have some control over the quality of your life before death. These are issues you might talk about with your doctors, family, and friends.

PRACTICAL DETAILS

If death is a possibility, there may be some very real, practical things you'll want to discuss and do. You may have unfinished business with people, or conversations that you want to have. You may want to discuss the effect of your death on your family. You may want to leave letters or tape recordings for young children or friends you haven't been able to talk to because of logistics or emotions.

You may have business or financial matters to take care of and you may need to pass on information and skills to other members of your family. You may want to take care of legal matters to convey your wishes and assure that they will be followed. The main legal documents you should consider are:

1) **Will.** The will stipulates who will receive your estate (money and possessions) and also who will care for any minor children. The formal will can be supplemented by a more detailed (but unofficial and thus and more easily amended) letter of instructions for your executor or your heirs.

2) **Power of Attorney for Health Care.** This is a crucial document that stipulates who can make medical decisions for you if you should become unable to make them. This document is respected in all states and is a concrete, legal means of spelling out your wishes. It allows the person you select to help you get what you want while also alleviating them of guilt and the responsibility of deciding for you.

3) **Living Will.** This document states your wishes about life support systems but is not legally recognized in all states. It is not a substitute for a Power of Attorney for Health Care.

4) **Do Not Resuscitate order** (DNR). This might be useful to ask your doctor about in certain cases. It stipulates that you are not to be brought back to life if your heart or breathing stop.

5) **General Power of Attorney.** This appoints a person of your choosing to make legal decisions and carry on business in your

name. This is essential if you become incapacitated but can be useful even if you aren't.

Many of these are standard forms, available in stationary stores and hospitals. For more on wills, see your library or bookstore.

Thinking about the practical things ahead of time doesn't at all preclude fighting to live — and ironically may allow you to concentrate more on living, knowing that if death should come you're not completely unprepared.

PLAN THE TIME THAT REMAINS

If everyone's best guess is that you only have about a year (or two months) to live, decide how you'd like to spend that time. What are the alternatives open to you? What are your resources? Don't assume there are things you can't do. There may be, of course, but don't begin with that assumption — check it all out.

Would you rather spend the year being pampered in your house or in a nursing home, or fill up on painkillers and travel to distant places, or continue your regular life and work as much as possible, or go live quietly in the country? Would you rather be as pain free as possible or as lucid as possible, even if that means tolerating some pain? Would you rather do everything possible to prolong your life or would you rather spend whatever time and energy you have doing other things than fighting your illness? Are there places you want to go before you die, people you want to talk with or be with? Are there things you want to do?

When my father was terminally ill, I asked him what he'd like to do if he could do anything he wanted. He replied he'd like to visit Paris, where he'd lived as a young man. He was old, with a bad heart, but he could still walk short distances and enjoy everything around him. He knew his physical limitations and all he wanted to do was to sit in Paris cafes and walk a few blocks down streets that he loved. His doctor had no medical objections to the trip and was quite supportive. I was willing to take him if my mother didn't want to go. In the end, he never went to Paris because my mother was afraid he might die while there and vetoed the trip. My father knew that risk and said he wouldn't mind dying in Paris, but he also wasn't willing to oppose his wife so he never took his trip. I wish he'd been able to realize his fantasy.

Another woman I knew, who had terminal cancer with about two years to live, gave up her apartment in the city, didn't tell her grown children of her diagnosis, and spent the next two years traveling. When the illness finally caught up with her, she came back, went into the hospital, and died shortly thereafter. But she had two wonderful years.

Another friend spent his last few months making his peace with dying at an early age. He spent as much time as possible with his children and friends, although most lived far away. He was weak but went on occasional drives to the mountains or a ball game when he felt up to it. Working closely with doctors and other healers, he was able to remain alert and relatively pain free until he died peacefully at home, surrounded by family and friends.

Friends can sometimes make a big difference in this period before death. When my friend Carl found out he was dying of AIDS and only had a few months to live, he very much wanted to finish a book he was writing. He asked his friends for help and they worked on the book together before his death.

Everybody makes different choices. Some stories are colorful and catch our imagination — but they might not be right for you. The choice itself isn't as important as the fact that *you* make it, that you decide what you want to do rather than just following a path out of lack of vision, lack of alternatives, or out of fear.

SUICIDE AND EUTHANASIA

"I have an enormous fear of either of us dying in a hospital. It's an absolute hatred of being in that kind of deadly, sterile surroundings."

Some people, for a variety or reasons, want to choose how and when they'll die — and for this reason some people think about euthanasia or suicide. I'm not talking about people who are suicidal because of depression, but rather about people already facing death due to old age or a terminal illness.

I know this is an uncomfortable topic for some people and one that raises controversial moral issues, but I mention it because there are many people, especially older people, who think about this a lot. Although the moral questions are for each person to decide, I raise the issue here in the hope that if it's relevant for you or someone in your family, you will discuss it. (For those interested in more information, see Hemlock Society founder Derek Humphry's, *Final Exit*.)

LETTING GO

There are times when acceptance of reality means accepting death, and the letting go of life that accompanies it.

How do you decide to let go of life and really prepare for death? It's not always simple and there are no easy answers, but at some point, unless death comes unexpectedly, you may have to face "letting go" of life. Sometimes there's a valid reason to hang on a little longer; sometimes we're just unable to let go and allow nature to take its course.

Family and friends also have to learn to let go. Often the person who is sick is ready to let go but a spouse, child, or parent isn't — which sometimes causes needless suffering for the person they claim to love.

And remember that we all die sometime; we can't change that. But we can control how we live our lives.

RIPPLES:

Effects on Family and Friends

RIPPLES

You drop a pebble into a pond. There is the first splash where it dropped but there are also ripples that go out from the center and touch every corner of the pond — and then sometimes turn around and come back, crossing other ripples.

Illness certainly has a great effect on the person who is sick — but it also has what I call a ripple effect on everyone around the sick person. Although this will vary with the nature of the illness, it's worth looking at more closely. And it's especially worth looking at since part of the problem for family and friends is that they're *not* the sick ones — so they and others may feel that their needs and feelings are less important. The needs and problems of family and friends are too often neglected.

"In many ways I think it's often harder emotionally for people who are close to the person who's sick than it is for the person himself." [from a man dying of cancer]

I heard that repeated many times in my conversations with people who were ill. I also talked with many friends and relatives and spent long hours hearing their perspectives and their problems. But who has the hardest time isn't really the issue. What is certain is that illness affects not just the sick person — but family, friends, and even slight acquaintances as well.

"One day I was waiting by the elevator and one of the volunteer ladies put her hand on me and said, 'My dear, you look very sad, do you have a sick person here?' and I just started to cry because nobody had asked. I told her and she just hugged me. Later she made a point to peek in the room once a

*day to see how I was, more than how Ruth was. She was a
very nice lady."*

The sick person usually has center stage. In most people's
eyes, his or her needs come first. The needs of friends and family
are perhaps secondary — but they're also often ignored, unmet,
unrecognized, or not seen as legitimate. Acquaintances usually get
left out completely; no one thinks about them. Yet the illness of
even a distant friend can touch off many emotions.

Friends and family are sometimes under so much stress that
they in turn need people to care for them. Because they're not
sick, however, they may feel guilty about asking for what they
need. Or they may simply not realize they are in need, or what
they need.

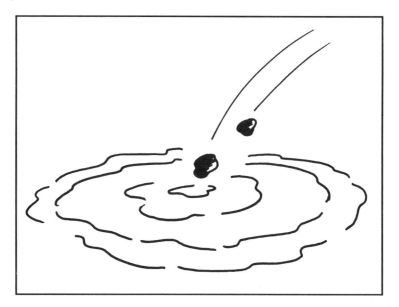

Just as ripples that reach the edge of a pond turn around and
go back to the center, so will the emotional well-being of family
and friends in turn affect the person who is sick.

FATIGUE AND STRAIN

Illness can cause a lot of tension and strain for friends and
relatives, whether the sick person is in the hospital or whether he
or she is being cared for at home. Home care can be especially
exhausting for the caregivers.

> *"There were nights when I got up 6-8 times during the night, putting on hot compresses, massaging her legs."* [from a teenage daughter]

> *"I didn't have any more space in me, anymore space to give."*

Hospital visits present another problem. The first several days my father was in the hospital (across the country from where I lived), I was allowed to see him for five minutes at noon and five minutes in the evening. I was staying an hour away, so I would commute two hours to see him for five minutes, then wander around the city all afternoon to see him for another five minutes in the evening. Even when the hospital is nearby, frequent visits can be very disruptive and draining.

> *"I just can't come to the hospital to see him every day. There's three kids at home and who's going to take care of them. I know he misses me but I just can't do it."*

> *"After a couple weeks of going to the hospital every day, I came home one evening crying all the way and I pulled up outside and I sat in the car, crying, and then finally yelled at the top of my lungs, 'I can't do this anymore, I can't go back there any more, I can't go on this way.' I came inside and made a fire and got stoned and admitted to myself that I didn't have the energy to go on, that I wasn't taking care of myself, that I was totally exhausted. I just couldn't do it.... I felt like I was just on a non-stop downhill roller-coaster and I was really going to crash. And when I did I wasn't going to be able to take care of anything. It was very scary, the sense of being totally out of control."* [from the wife of a man dying of pancreatic cancer]

Just the related problems, the life changes caused by illness, and the need or family members to take on new roles and duties, can create tremendous pressure.

> *"In some ways it made us closer and in others it raised tensions. Nora was suddenly not earning anything, she was totally dependent on me. There was the threat of all the bills and medical stuff, there was our daughter to take care of, plus all the pre-existing pressures which were already enormous. I was right up to the edge of what I could handle, in fact I was sort of over what I could handle."* [from a man whose wife had a badly broken leg]

As friends and family feel more strain, they are likely to have less energy for the other things they normally do and the other people they deal with — at home, work, and play.

It has long been accepted in the helping professions that helpers need help too. A therapist who listens to the troubles of others all day can become physically and emotionally drained and needy. Therapists often have consultants, co-workers, or their own psychologists to share the strain with — not to mention the role their family and friends play. Non-professionals have the same needs although they often don't have a support network in place or even the recognition of that need. The energy drain of a sick person in the family will make other family members more needy — and they may turn to *their* friends and family, or therapists if they have them, for more of the support they need. They may need a chance to talk, patience, understanding, or just a hug. They may also need practical help with chores or with life's regular duties — such as time off from work, a lower workload, extra babysitting, grocery shopping, or meal preparation.

The friend or relative who previously had extra energy to give to others, may now consume all he or she has. This can show up in various ways. You may no longer have the energy to play with the kids; or the time to listen to their problems or joys; the concentration to do your job; or the patience to put up with the neighbor's dog, the kids' squabbling, or frustrations at work.

In the normal course of life, we often get used to getting our everyday emotional needs met in certain ways. We look to our spouse, parents, children, or friends. What happens when all of a sudden a person we rely on for that becomes ill and needs us — and is less able to meet our needs. All of a sudden there may be a void and we don't know quite where to turn to fill it. Perhaps we won't even be aware of our increased needs — and/or have no way to get them met.

"All I knew was my boyfriend was in the hospital — drowsy and exhausted most of the time — and scared. He couldn't help me. I just wanted to be held and feel loved. I was scared too."

Although the person who's sick may not be able to meet the needs of others, that may also *not* be true. The sick person may be *very* able to give, and may even be delighted to be asked. It may even be important for them to do so — a chance to feel useful, a chance perhaps for them to give at a time when they may feel they are a burden on others.

Sometimes the problem is that the person who's well is unable or unwilling to ask for anything from the sick person or to let the sick person be of help in any way. The moral: let sick people be of use for emotional and practical needs if they want and are able to be.

BURNOUT

Burnout is a problem for anyone facing heavy demands and a lot of stress. If you're aware of this, you can take steps ahead of time to prevent it.

"I was working full time and with a house and daughter and trying to get down to the hospital every day. I almost didn't see in time that I was just burning myself out. I found myself beginning to get angry at Tony. It was horrible."

Ask for help from family and friends. Check out the services available from your nearest hospice, including "respite care" that allows caregivers to have time off. Although specific services vary with each hospice, and they are limited to patients who are dying, the hospice organization provides a good model for the kinds of services that are needed. It would be helpful to have them available for all illnesses.

INVOLUNTARY HELPERS

Often relatives and friends are more than willing to be of assistance — but that's not always not the case. You may have little contact with, or perhaps even dislike, certain relatives. Or you may love the person dearly but have other pressing priorities in your life, such as your own family or work, that prevent you from becoming too involved with the person who's sick. And some people, although they may want to help, just can't deal with illness.

If a close relative gets sick, it's not easy to say, "No, thank you, I'd rather not help."

"As a kid I always had to take care of my mother when she was sick at home. It wasn't anything I ever wanted to do, it was almost required of me. I was the oldest girl and she would ask me to do it. How do you say 'no' to your mother when she needs an enema."

Sometimes a caregiver didn't really want to be in that role in the first place, or they may discover too late that they've taken on more than they bargained for. These situations are never easy and sometimes there are no viable alternatives and you just have to do your best in the situation. But at other times you can admit the arrangement doesn't work and explore alternatives. Ask for help from other family members and friends, as well as from the medical team and any relevant government or private agencies.

Illness often brings people into closer contact with other relatives or friends. That may be very pleasant if all the people get along well, but painful if there are old conflicts and difficulties among them. The illness may create new problems or intensify old ones. Relatives may disagree on the best course of treatment, who is to care for the sick person, or how to pay for the treatment.

ADVOCATES

Sometimes the person who is ill will need or want a family member or friend to serve as their advocate. Young children, the very old, those who can't speak English, or those too sick to participate in their care may be unable to ask for what they need or sometimes even to say what hurts. They will need someone to speak for them. Family and friends may have to interpret (at the very least) and sometimes even guess what the sick person needs and wants. This is both difficult — and a heavy responsibility. It may also require good detective skills as well as an intimate knowledge of the sick person.

When my mother's memory began to fail, I took over total responsibility for her care. Between her natural passivity, her lack of medical sophistication, and her long and short-term memory loss, it was very difficult for me to know what the problem was. When the doctor would ask her what the problem was, she'd reply, "You're the doctor, you tell me." I found myself testing theories, often unsure if there was a specific problem that could be remedied or if she was just getting old. At one point, as she became more disoriented and unsteady on her feet, I wondered if her vision was part of the problem, although she never mentioned it. Removing a cataract helped considerably.

CHILDREN

Illness of a member of the family can be especially difficult and even terrifying for children.

"I have a child, and who's parenting her? I'm ill — and her father feels really inadequate. She started wetting her bed and showing a lot of anxiety. We took her to see a child therapist. The therapist told us she had tremendous coping skills but she had a terror of being alone and abandoned."

"Our girls, who were always really nice little girls, really reacted strongly. They were clearly acting out. I've read since then that it very often happens. Here you think the kids are going to be really good and helpful and understanding. But they were doing all kinds of really strange things. They were probably scared to death." [from a man who had a heart attack]

Children may be discouraged or actually banned from visiting at the hospital or the hospital may be located far from friends and family. In this situation, the children who are cut off from the sick person may be left to imagine the worst and may feel abandoned.

Some kids have new responsibilities thrust upon them — to help care for a sick person or to take more responsibility for themselves or other siblings because the adults are now too busy.

"When my mother went into the hospital, I was the surrogate mother. I'd have to make all the meals for everyone, keep the house clean, plus worry about why she was sick.... It just cut out being a kid. If you're in grade school, you're not that quick at cooking and doing the laundry and we had a fairly big house, and four kids and my father and the dog. I got home from school in the late afternoon and it took most of my day that was left to do all of those things. That took away from play time and that pretty much wiped out a big chunk of my childhood. I wasn't a child, I was a mother."

When there's illness in a family, some people get ignored. Or they're told explicitly that their needs are not as important and just won't or can't be met right then. Kids often suffer a lot from this. There may not be any time to plan a birthday party, to take a child to play with a friend or to the zoo, or to hear about a teenager's first love. Parents may become oblivious to the daily lives of other members of the family.

"My daughter was 15 and just discovering boys and seeing herself as a young lady. It was a crucial time for her and she needed me — but I was too preoccupied with my illness to notice." [from a woman with bone cancer]

Or there may simply be little tolerance for the natural noise of children.

"You couldn't play, you had to be quiet. It was a very disruptive thing to have her home."

Children can also learn and grow from being around illness. They may benefit from greater independence and an increased sense of responsibility. They may learn from watching others cope with a difficult situation. If they're involved in caring for the sick person, they may receive much love and appreciation. There are many practical things children can do to help, depending on their age and abilities.

If children are involved, don't assume these positive interactions will just occur naturally — encourage them. For everyone's sake, including the children, try to maintain some familiar family life: tell bedtime stories, celebrate birthdays and holidays, watch a movie together, shop for new school clothes, go on a fishing trip or for a walk.

PRACTICAL SIDE EFFECTS

As we've already discussed, a major or prolonged illness will generally cause changes in the lives of friends and relatives, as well as in the life of the person who is ill. All the general changes we looked at earlier in Chapter 13 — changes in living situation, work, income, financial priorities, and redistributed work load — are bound to affect the whole family, as well as just the person who's sick. Those changes, even without any illness, would create new tensions and problems for the family.

When a sick person is forced to give up his or her home and move in with relatives, it affects everyone, even when the sick relative is welcome and there's enough room (which isn't always the case). A sick person in the home may change the tone of the house. There may be a palpable sense of worry and stress in the air. The house may have a "sick" smell and feeling. Visitors may come at all hours, decreasing privacy and perhaps creating even more work — or friends may stay away. All this causes disruption in the lives of more than just the sick person, even if the changes are agreed to by all members of the family. Children or even spouses who had no voice in the decision will still be affected by it.

If the sick person is in a hospital, then family members may spend much time away from their homes. Kids may see very little of their parents. Adults may see very little of their friends and loved ones, precisely the people from whom they could get comfort and support. People may have to miss work and forego meetings, vacations, parties, visits with friends or other things they would normally do. Life ceases being "normal." You can make an effort to minimize the disruption, but some is inevitable.

One image we have of illness is of a tired but cheerful old woman propped up in bed wearing full make-up and a new nightgown, surrounded by gorgeous flowers and the smell of roses and lilacs. But illness can also be ugly and mean bedpans, bed sores, tubes, green bile, and sickly hospital smells. And perhaps neediness, depression, and anger. Sometimes friends and family find they have to deal with things they were never really prepared for.

EMOTIONS: FRIENDS AND FAMILY

Illness can touch off the same emotions for family and friends that it does for the person who is sick. Let's look briefly at fear, powerlessness, aloneness, anger, and guilt as they apply to family and friends. (For more on these emotions — and ideas for how to deal with them — see Chapters 4-11.)

POWERLESSNESS

Powerless feelings are as common for families as for those who are sick. Friends and families have even less control over the illness than does the sick person — and it's very frustrating not to be able to make someone you love get better.

"What am I supposed to do? And if I'm not able to do it, then am I failing in the relationship? Obviously I'm helpless in the situation. I can give her moral support. I can hold her, I can give her very important things. But in medical terms, I can't do anything. I can't take care of her except in certain emotional ways. So that strips me of my manhood, on a certain level."

"The kind of feeling I've had with Bud's illness has been a helplessness. I wanted to do something but couldn't do anything about it. I wanted to fix it for him."

Illness definitely frustrates our natural desires to "make it all better."

FEAR

Some of the fears of friends and relatives are the same as for the person who is sick — fear of death, loss, the unknown, abandonment.

The person who is ill or dying is not the only person who fears death. It's also a great fear for family and friends.

"Maybe it's easy for me to say this because I'm healthy, but I'm more upset by someone else dying, someone close to me, than the thought that I might die. If someone close to me dies, I'll feel that loss a lot."

Death is a real loss. Who, or what, will take the place of the person who is dying?

"He's the one who's dying — but I have such a terrible fear of being abandoned, which is what he feels too sometimes. He's afraid I'll abandon him before he dies. I'm afraid he'll abandon me when he dies."

"When my husband had the heart attack — I panicked. He dealt with it much better that I did. He was in many ways ready to die. He felt he'd had a good, full life. But I wasn't at all ready for him to die. I didn't know what I would do without him"

Death often has other implications, especially for those who will take over the responsibilities of the person who died — and that can be another source of fear.

"I was panicked originally at the thought of taking care of myself. I'd never done that." [from an older woman whose husband was dying]

"It was always very scary. She was always being anointed by the priest and they thought she was going to die. That was just awful, not only because I would lose my mother, but I'm

sure I thought I'd always have to do all the housekeeping and take care of my sister and that certainly wasn't very pleasant."

"I haven't really panicked around Mary, but I have gotten frightened. She's got a lot that she's responsible for — two young kids, a house, mortgages, all of it. She's responsible for an amazing amount more than I've ever been. If there's some kind of implicit threat that that responsibility might be turned over to me, my big strong American male instinct is to run! It's scary!" [from a man about to marry a woman with a potentially serious illness.]

"I worried about a lot of things when Sarah was dying... who's going to pay the bills, what about the tax stuff, who's going to do the laundry, who's going to clean the house."

Some fears can come as a flip side to the emotions of the sick person. Their anger can lead to our fear that they may leave us, their deep depressions may make us fear their suicide, their dependency may make us afraid of being overwhelmed.

Some fear is caused by the very real needs of the sick person, and the demands that puts on friends and relatives. How do you take care of someone who's ill? What do they need? What if they need something you can't give? What if you can't ease the pain? What if there's an emergency and you don't know what to do?

"Simply watching someone who is sick can be frightening for the observer, especially someone not used to illness."

"Ted was frightened. He was not only frightened; he didn't know how to act around such a thing. To have a helpless young wife on his hands was pretty overwhelming." [from a woman who had a serious arm infection]

"The enormity of the pain is just something to behold. It's scary. And it's scary to watch."

And, as with the person who's ill, fear can have many gradations, from simple worry to panic. As a young child put it:

"I don't like you having doctor's appointments while I'm at school because it makes me wonder all day long."

And perhaps that makes her pay less attention to her schoolwork, and thus get lower grades, and.... Ripples.

ALONENESS

People who are sick often feel isolated and alone — but their relatives can also have those feelings. At least the sick person usually gets attention and gets waited on: not so for relatives.

> *"I felt a loneliness that I haven't really experienced before, that came from thinking he's not really available to me. And that's what dying means, and it's permanent."* [from a woman whose husband had terminal cancer]

> *"With Frances in the hospital, I feel scattered and just sort of lost. I don't know what to do. We've never been so much apart. I go to the hospital to visit her twice a day. I don't cook anything. I've got some eggs that have been in the refrigerator so long they'd hatch if they'd been kept warm. It seems like I can't settle down. It's a really bad scene for the people who aren't in the hospital."* [from an older man whose wife was in the hospital for a few weeks with heart problems]

Illness that may end in death raises other issues of aloneness and abandonment. When my friend Mimi was close to death, she said, "I'll miss you." "No, that's just it," I replied, "You won't be around to miss me, but I'll still be here and you won't be around to talk to."

Families are all too often ignored by doctors and hospital personnel, adding to their aloneness.

> *"I saw the doctor running by and I tried to catch him and he said he was too busy. I was really upset. I felt so isolated."*

> *"No one talking to the family is really bad. You're made to feel in the way."*

Doctors should seek to include families as part of the team, not only because the families have real needs, but also because the help and support of families can be so important for the patient.

ANGER

Anger may be linked to these feelings of helplessness and frustration. And, again, the person who is sick isn't always the only one who's angry.

> *"Her being sick always hung over us, even when she would come back from the hospital. I would be really happy to see her*

but I expected her to be healed, and when she came home and was still sick and still needed a lot of taking care of, then I would get really angry and would start having fights with her, usually the first day she got home, because then not only did I have to do all these other chores but I also had to take care of her....I guess I either wanted her healthy or not at all." [from a woman who cared for her mother often as a young child]

"I got very angry at her when I saw her doing stuff that I perceived as life-threatening to her."

Sometimes relatives and friends keep their anger bottled inside — but sometimes it gets expressed:

"I exploded. 'You can't continue to demand as much of me as you demand because I can't do it'."

"She announced to me in a tirade that she thought I was trying to make her life as miserable as I could. I was astonished. I was aghast. I threw her crutches around the room and I threw a lot of other things around the room and said it was absolutely too much. Both of us separated in tears."

Often, however, the anger is not expressed. After all, how angry can you get at someone who is sick? After talking about how her husband's illness affected her, one woman said:

"I was beginning to get very angry. But how could I? He's lying there helpless in a hospital bed and I'm angry at him. We had also just found out for sure that he had cancer."

GUILT

The honest feelings of friends and relatives are difficult enough to deal with — but often guilt is added on top. Family and friends feel certain things are expected of them in much the same way the sick person does.

"There were all these 'shoulds' on me and one of them was that I had to get down to the hospital every day and that I had to be supportive and understanding at all times and that I had to keep my own emotions subordinated."

"I feel guilty if I'm casually talking to somebody or enjoying myself. I should be suffering too."

We all have expectations of how we're supposed to act when someone is sick. We're supposed to be loving, helpful, and supportive — and hide our own needs and desires. After all, they're sick.

When my father was in the hospital and still very ill after his heart surgery, I felt that much was expected of me. The first week I felt I had to stay near a phone whenever I wasn't at the hospital. One night, desperate for diversion, I went with a friend to see a comedy double-feature. I felt guilty all through the movies. What if someone needed to reach me? More than that, how could I laugh when my father was so sick? And a double feature! It wasn't rational. I knew I really needed to get away from it all and laugh and relax, yet the guilt remained.

Sometimes the feelings around illness get very complicated, and are *not* what one might expect. Illness may be welcomed by the family in the same way it sometimes is by the patient (although they may not be able to feel the relief without a lot of guilt). The separation caused by hospitalization, for example, may be welcomed by a spouse or other family member who didn't know how to deal with an unbearable (or burdensome or unpleasant) situation in the home. We may be glad that someone is out of the home, even if it's because of illness. The house may be much more pleasant without the sick person. We may even wish they would die. That might be a solution to a lot of suffering for the sick person or for others. But that's not how we're "supposed" to feel, so there may also be guilt connected with those feelings.

We may feel especially guilty if we feel some responsibility for the illness. "Perhaps I caused my child's illness by letting her go out in the rain." "If I'd only taken her to the doctor sooner." "If only I hadn't urged my husband to take that job." "If I'd only paid more attention to that cough." The variations are endless.

> *"At times I felt she was sick because I had been bad. I'd go through all sorts of bargaining things with God — we were very devout Catholics. I would range from being very angry with Him and refusing to pray, to 'If you make my mother better, I'll say a rosary and I'll come to church every day.' I thought it was something I had done, because I was often disobedient."* [from the woman whose mother was often sick]

WHAT FRIENDS AND FAMILY CAN DO

There are many things family and friends can do to help them through the emotional stress and practical problems of an illness.

WHAT FRIENDS AND FAMILY CAN DO

1. Get help. Share the burdens.
2. Take care of yourself
3. Take care of each other.
4. Find ways to help the person who is sick.
5. Continue your life.

---

1. GET HELP

Get help and share the burdens as much as you can. Develop your own support network. Ask for practical and emotional support from both official circles (social workers, therapists, medical staff, support groups) and from friends and other family members.

2. TAKE CARE OF YOURSELF

Develop your own support network and take time for yourself. It's often helpful to share experiences and feelings with other caregivers. It may also be useful to get support from friends who are *not* dealing with the same sick person and who may therefore be less drained, have a clearer perspective, and simply not be overwhelmed with the same illness.

Pay special attention to the section called Help Yourself Heal (p. 59) and remember the "Big Four:" good nutrition, exercise, rest, and relaxation. Those are equally important for family and friends — and very easy to forget when your attention is focussed on someone else and there's way too much to do.

Set aside time for exercise. If you can't do that, walk briskly around the hospital, take stairs rather than the elevator, park at the far end of the parking lot, or get off the bus a few stops away. Hospital cafeterias often have fairly good food at reasonable prices. Eat there, if you can, rather than relying on vending machines. Treat yourself to a healthy meal as often as possible. If you can, take full days off, even vacations. Try to continue activities you enjoy, whether it's going to the movies, fishing, reading, or a bridge club. Set aside 15 minutes a day of quiet time. Leave the answering machine on. Learn meditation. Take a hot bath.

3. TAKE CARE OF EACH OTHER

Take care of each other. Ask others how they're holding up. If you're a more distant friend, help those who are in the thick of it. Offer to make dinner, give backrubs, baby-sit, or cover for them so they can have some time off.

4. HELP THE PERSON WHO IS SICK

There will always be things you can do to help the person who is sick — and that, in turn, will make you feel useful and less helpless. Ways of helping include all levels of skill and intimacy. I've already given many suggestions throughout the book but here's a quick review: make chicken soup, give massages or backrubs, run errands, change bandages, help fill out insurance forms, go for walks, research the illness or treatments, give a hug or hold a hand, cook healthy meals or special treats, wash hair, organize other friends to help, take the person to the doctor or shopping, take the dog for a walk, help with relaxation exercises or visualization, play cards, watch a movie together, or just talk and listen. Ask what they need and what they'd like from you.

5. CONTINUE YOUR LIFE

In addition to taking care of the sick person, family and friends need to continue to live their own lives and take care of themselves and each other. One woman, whose husband was dying of cancer, realized she was getting totally run down and vowed to:

"...make more time for myself — to run more, to go have saunas, and to sit alone by myself. And I wasn't going to answer the phone all the time. After that I didn't go there every day and I finally created a sort of equilibrium again and felt I was in charge of my own life."

And she continued:

"I now take care of myself in ways I didn't used to. I eat better, I get exercise, I try to do things that make me feel like my life is worthwhile — that's been the biggest change in my life. I suddenly realized that I had to stop living for the future. It makes me feel better about myself."

Life must go on.

PARTING WORDS

I hope this handbook has been of use — that it's given you a little more of a road map to follow as you navigate through an illness. I also hope this slow look at illness, through a microscope if you will, has demystified and helped shed some light on the many emotional effects an illness can have — and that it has given you ideas to deal with them productively. I hope it has also helped you to realize that there are many ways to make your experience with illness a better one and to help yourself get well.

I hope that perhaps I've even inspired you to take a more active role in your healing — both by sharing your feelings and by taking charge and exercising as much power and control as possible. I hope you'll be an active part of the team in your fight for health. And, perhaps most important, I hope that what you'll learn in relation to illness may also be of use in other parts of your life and that you may make your whole life as good as it can be.

APPENDIX

GLOSSARY

Acupuncture. A method of reducing pain or treating a condition by inserting thin needles into the skin at specific acupuncture points.

AMA. Against medical advice. (also the American Medical Association)

Analgesic. Pain-relieving, as in a drug that relieves pain. These can be either narcotic or non-narcotic (NSAIDs).

Antibiotic. A medicine which can kill or decrease the growth of bacteria and other microorganisms. Antibiotics must generally be taken for a specified period of time even though the symptoms may have disappeared) to be sure to kill all the bacteria.

Benign. Non-cancerous, non-malignant.

Chiropractic. A system that stresses the importance of the nervous system and in practice relies primarily on manipulation of the spinal column.

CT scan (computed tomography). A technique that uses a series of X-rays to show a detailed cross-section of tissue structure. Painless and non-invasive. (Also called CAT scan)

Dementia. A progressive mental deterioration characterized by memory loss, confusion, and personality disintegration. Sometimes reversible and sometimes not, depending on the cause. Can be caused by various diseases, organic conditions, or drugs. Alzheimer's disease is one type of dementia.

Depression. An emotional state characterized by feelings of sadness, despair, discouragement, and, if serious, hopelessness and worthlessness. Depression can be mild, a response in proportion to a loss or tragedy, or severe, where the feelings are exaggerated and out of proportion, or unrelated, to reality.

DNR. Do not resuscitate. An order to doctors not to resuscitate someone in case of cardiac or respiratory failure.

ECG (also **EKG**). Electrocardiogram. Measures heart function.

ER. Emergency room.

Euthanasia. (From the Greek, "good death"). Deliberately, either actively or passively (by withholding treatment) bringing about the death of a person who is suffering from an incurable illness.

Generic drug. A drug that is not protected by a trademark. Generic drugs use the name officially assigned to the compound.

HMO (health maintenance organization). A group health practice that provides medical services to its members for a fixed fee regardless of the services rendered, as opposed to "fee for service" where you pay for each service received.

Homeopathy. A therapeutic system which uses very small doses of drugs to treat a disease, drugs that in larger doses could cause symptoms of that disease.

ICU. Intensive care unit. For seriously ill patients needing extra monitoring and care.

Immune system. The network of white blood cells and antibodies and other chemicals that the body produces to protect itself against infection and disease. The immune system recognizes and attacks anything it determines to be non-self.

Internist. A doctor who specializes in disorders of the internal organs, commonly a primary care physician.

IV (intravenous). Into a vein. Can refer to a drug injected into a vein or an IV line (tube) inserted into a vein, usually for the purpose of introducing medication.

Lumpectomy. Surgical removal of a tumor only, without removing large amounts of surrounding tissue. Often used for breast cancer.

Malignant. Tending to spread and cause death, as in a cancerous tumor.

Mammogram. A low-dose X-ray of the breast.

Mastectomy. Removal of a breast, usually to remove a malignant tumor.

Metastasis. The spreading of tumor cells spread to distant parts of the body, as in cancer.

MRI (magnetic resonance imagery). A process that uses radio-frequency radiation to show images of the body.

NPO (*nolo per orifice,* nothing by mouth). Take neither food nor drink, a standard procedure before surgery.

Oncologist. A doctor who specialized in cancer.

OR. Operating room

Orphan drug. A drug that has not been "adopted" for distribution in the U.S. due to financial (not enough people would use it to justify research and development costs), regulatory (not approved by the Food and Drug Administration), or political reasons.

Ostomy. A surgical opening created to allow urine or stool to empty through the abdominal wall into a special pouch.

PCA (patient controlled analgesia). A pump that allows the patient to push a button which releases a predetermined amount of medication into an IV line.

PDR (Physicians' Desk Reference). A book that lists all prescription drugs and their effects and side-effects.

Psychiatrist. A medical doctor who specializes in emotional problems, especially including their chemical component, and can prescribe medications.

Psychologist. A person with graduate training in dealing with emotional problems but not a medical doctor and not able to prescribe medication.

Psychoneuroimmunology (PNI). The study of the relationship between psychology, neurology, and immunology — in other words, the relationship between our minds and our bodies, primarily the immune system (I prefer psycho-neuro-immunology).

PRN (*pro re nata,* as circumstances require). Use as needed, as in a medication or treatment.

Placebo. An inactive or ineffective substance given as if it were an effective dose of medication. (From the Latin, "shall please.")

Prosthesis. An artificial replacement for a missing part of the body, such as an arm, leg, hip, or breast.

Triage. A process by which patients are sorted and prioritized according to their need for care. Used in war, natural disasters, and emergency rooms.

Ultrasound. A process that uses high-frequency sound waves for imaging internal organs or for healing.

X-ray. A process that uses electromagnetic radiation for imaging parts of the body or destroying diseased tissue.

RESOURCES

ORGANIZATIONS

The following are some of the major health organizations. The *Encyclopedia of Associations* (Gale Research, Inc), found in most libraries, has a comprehensive list. Check your local phone book, there may be a chapter of these organizations or other local groups near you.

Alzheimer's Association: 919 N. Michigan Ave. (#1000) Chicago, Il, 60611 (312) 335-8700, (800) 272-3900

American Cancer Society: 1599 Clifton Rd., N.E., Atlanta, GA 30329 (800) ACS-2345

American Chronic Pain Association: P.O. Box 850, Rocklin, CA 95677 (916) 632-0922

American Diabetes Association: P.O. Box 25757, Alexandria, VA 22314 (800) DIABETES

American Heart Association: 7272 Greenville Ave., Dallas, TX 75231 (800) 242-8721

American Self-Help Clearinghouse: St. Clares-Riverside Medical Center, Denville, NJ 07834 (201) 625-7101 (has lists of self-help groups and state clearinghouses)

Arthritis Foundation: 1314 Spring St., N.W., Atlanta GA 30309 (800) 283-7800

Choice in Dying: 200 Varick St., New York, NY 10014 (212) 366-5540, (800) 989-9455

Hemlock Society USA: P.O. Box 11830, Eugene, OR 97440 (503) 342-5748

National Multiple Sclerosis Society: 733 3rd Ave., New York, NY 10017 (800) 344-4867

Muscular Dystrophy Association: 3300 E. Sunrise Dr., Tucson, AZ 85718   (602) 529-2000, (800) 572-1717

National AIDS Clearinghouse (CDC): P.O. Box 6003, Rockville, MD 20849   (800) 458-5231

National AIDS Hotline: (800) 342-2437

National Headache Foundation: 5252 N Western Ave, Chicago, IL 60625   (800) 843-2256

National Hospice Organization: 1901 N Moore St, Arlington, VA 22209   (800) 658-8898

National Organization for Rare Disorders: P.O. Box 8923, New Fairfield, CT   06812   (800) 999-NORD

National Stroke Association: 8480 E. Orchard Rd. (#1000) Englewood, CO 80111   (303) 771-1700, (800) STROKES

United Cerebral Palsy Associations: 1660 L St. N.W. (#700), Washington, D.C. 20036   (202) 842-1266, (800) 872-5827

United Ostomy Association: 36 Executive Park (#120), Irvine, CA   92714   (714) 660-8624, (800) 826-0826

BOOKS

Herbert Benson, *The Relaxation Response* (1975)
Norman Cousins, *Anatomy of an Illness* (1979), *The Healing Heart* (1983), and *Head First* (1984)
Helen Garvy, *The Immune System: Your Magic Doctor* (1992)
Derek Humphry, *Final Exit* (1991)
Jon Kabat-Zinn, *Full Catastrophe Living* (1990)
Elizabeth Kübler-Ross, *On Death and Dying* (1969)
Stephen Locke and Douglas Colligan, *The Healer Within* (1986)
Susan Love, *Dr. Susan Love's Breast Book* (1990)
"Our Immune System: The Wars Within," *National Geographic*, Vol. 169, No. 6, June 1986
Mike Samuels and Hal Bennett, The Well Body Book (1973)
O. Carl Simonton, Stephanie Matthews-Simonton, and James Creighton, *Getting Well Again* (1978)

INDEX

DATE DUE

ORDER FORM

If you can't find *Coping With Illness* in your local bookstore, additional copies are available from Shire Press.

Also available: ***The Immune System: Your Magic Doctor*** by Helen Garvy. An illustrated book for children — and the curious of all ages. Recommended by *Science Books and Films* as one of the best children's science books of 1992. (Full color; 76 pages; hardback, $15; paperback, $12)

* *

_____ *Coping With Illness* ($12)   _____

_____ *The Immune System: Your Magic Doctor*

(hardback — $15)   _____
(paperback — $12   _____

postage and handling ($1.50/book) _____

TOTAL _____

Send books to:

_____

_____

_____

Please enclose payment with your order. California residents add sales tax.

SHIRE PRESS 26873 Hester Creek Road, Los Gatos, CA 95030